Lillian Hellman

Lillian Hellman

SAUNDRA TOWNS

CHELSEA HOUSE PUBLISHERS

NEW YORK · PHILADELPHIA

Chelsea House Publishers
EDITOR-IN-CHIEF Nancy Toff
EXECUTIVE EDITOR Remmel T. Nunn
MANAGING EDITOR Karyn Gullen Browne
COPY CHIEF Juliann Barbato
PICTURE EDITOR Adrian G. Allen
ART DIRECTOR Maria Epes
MANUFACTURING MANAGER Gerald Levine

American Women of Achievement
SENIOR EDITOR Constance Jones

Staff for Lillian Hellman
ASSOCIATE EDITOR Maria Behan
COPY EDITOR Lisa S. Fenev
DEPUTY COPY CHIEF Nicole Bowen
EDITORIAL ASSISTANT Claire Wilson
PICTURE RESEARCHER Andrea Reithmayr
ASSISTANT ART DIRECTOR Loraine Machlin
DESIGNER Donna Sinisgalli
PRODUCTION COORDINATOR Joseph Romano
COVER ART Bryn Barnard
COVER ORNAMENT Loraine Machlin

J 92
HELLMAN

1 3 5 7 9 8 6 4 2

Library of Congress Cataloging-in-Publication Data

Towns, Saundra. LILLIAN HELLMAN.

(American women of achievement)
Bibliography: p.
Includes index.
Summary: Examines the career of Lillian Hellman, including
her early life, making as a playwright, and involvement in poli-
tics.
    1. Hellman, Lillian, 1906–   —Biography—Juvenile
literature. 2. Dramatists, American—20th century—
Biography—Juvenile literature. [1. Hellman, Lillian,
1906–   . 2. Authors, American] I. Title.
II. Series.
PS3515.E343Z9 1989   812'.52 [B] [92]   88-35347
ISBN 1-55546-657-5
    0-7910-0437-6 (pbk.)

CONTENTS

AMERICAN WOMEN OF ACHIEVEMENT

Abigail Adams
women's rights advocate

Jane Addams
social worker

Louisa May Alcott
author

Marian Anderson
singer

Susan B. Anthony
woman suffragist

Ethel Barrymore
actress

Clara Barton
*founder of the American
Red Cross*

Elizabeth Blackwell
physician

Nellie Bly
journalist

Margaret Bourke-White
photographer

Pearl Buck
author

Rachel Carson
biologist and author

Mary Cassatt
artist

Agnes De Mille
choreographer

Emily Dickinson
poet

Isadora Duncan
dancer

Amelia Earhart
aviator

Mary Baker Eddy
*founder of the Christian
Science church*

Betty Friedan
feminist

Althea Gibson
tennis champion

Emma Goldman
political activist

Helen Hayes
actress

Lillian Hellman
playwright

Katharine Hepburn
actress

Karen Horney
psychoanalyst

Anne Hutchinson
religious leader

Mahalia Jackson
gospel singer

Helen Keller
humanitarian

Jeane Kirkpatrick
diplomat

Emma Lazarus
poet

Clare Boothe Luce
author and diplomat

Barbara McClintock
biologist

Margaret Mead
anthropologist

Edna St. Vincent Millay
poet

Julia Morgan
architect

Grandma Moses
painter

Louise Nevelson
sculptor

Sandra Day O'Connor
Supreme Court justice

Georgia O'Keeffe
painter

Eleanor Roosevelt
diplomat and humanitarian

Wilma Rudolph
champion athlete

Florence Sabin
medical researcher

Beverly Sills
opera singer

Gertrude Stein
author

Gloria Steinem
feminist

Harriet Beecher Stowe
author and abolitionist

Mae West
entertainer

Edith Wharton
author

Phillis Wheatley
poet

Babe Didrikson Zaharias
champion athlete

CHELSEA HOUSE PUBLISHERS

"REMEMBER THE LADIES"

MATINA S. HORNER

Remember the Ladies." That is what Abigail Adams wrote to her husband, John, then a delegate to the Continental Congress, as the Founding Fathers met in Philadelphia to form a new nation in March of 1776. "Be more generous and favorable to them than your ancestors. Do not put such unlimited power in the hands of the Husbands. If particular care and attention is not paid to the Ladies," Abigail Adams warned, "we are determined to foment a Rebellion, and will not hold ourselves bound by any Laws in which we have no voice, or Representation."

The words of Abigail Adams, one of the earliest American advocates of women's rights, were prophetic. Because when we have not "remembered the ladies," they have, by their words and deeds, reminded us so forcefully of the omission that we cannot fail to remember them. For the history of American women is as interesting and varied as the history of our nation as a whole. American women have played an integral part in founding, settling, and building our country. Some we remember as remarkable women who—against great odds—achieved distinction in the public arena: Anne Hutchinson, who in the 17th century became a charismatic religious leader; Phillis Wheatley, an 18th-century black slave who became a poet; Susan B. Anthony, whose name is synonymous with the 19th-century women's rights movement and who led the struggle to enfranchise women; and, in our own century, Amelia Earhart, the first woman to cross the Atlantic Ocean by air.

These extraordinary women certainly merit our admiration, but other women, "common women," many of them all but forgotten, should also be recognized for their contributions to American thought and culture. Women have been community builders; they have founded schools and formed voluntary associations to help those in need; they have assumed the major responsibility for rearing children, passing on from one generation to the next the values that keep a culture alive. These and innumerable other contributions, once ignored, are now being recognized by scholars, students, and the public. It is exciting and gratifying to realize that a part of our history that was hardly acknowledged a few generations ago is now being studied and brought to light.

In recent decades, the field of women's history has grown from obscurity to a politically controversial splinter movement to academic respectability, in many cases mainstreamed into such traditional disciplines as history, economics, and psychology. Scholars of women, both female and male, have organized research centers at such prestigious institutions as Wellesley College, Stanford University, and the University of California. Other notable centers for women's studies are the Center for the American Woman and Politics at the Eagleton Institute of Politics at Rutgers University; the Henry A. Murray Research Center for the Study of Lives, at Radcliffe College; and the Women's Research and Education Institute, the research arm of the Congressional Caucus on Women's Issues. Other scholars and public figures have established archives and libraries, such as the Schlesinger Library on the History of Women in America, at Radcliffe College, and the Sophia Smith Collection, at Smith College, to collect and preserve the written and tangible legacies of women.

From the initial donation of the Women's Rights Collection in 1943, the Schlesinger Library grew to encompass vast collections documenting the manifold accomplishments of American women. Simultaneously, the women's movement in general and the academic discipline of women's studies in particular also began with a narrow definition and gradually expanded their mandate. Early causes such as woman suffrage and social reform, abolition and organized labor were joined by newer concerns such as the history of women in business and the professions and in politics and government; the study of the family; and social issues such as health policy and education.

Women, as historian Arthur M. Schlesinger, jr., once pointed out, "have constituted the most spectacular casualty of traditional history.

INTRODUCTION

They have made up at least half the human race, but you could never tell that by looking at the books historians write." The new breed of historians is remedying that omission. They have written books about immigrant women and about working-class women who struggled for survival in cities and about black women who met the challenges of life in rural areas. They are telling the stories of women who, despite the barriers of tradition and economics, became lawyers and doctors and public figures.

The women's studies movement has also led scholars to question traditional interpretations of their respective disciplines. For example, the study of war has traditionally been an exercise in military and political analysis, an examination of strategies planned and executed by men. But scholars of women's history have pointed out that wars have also been periods of tremendous change and even opportunity for women, because the very absence of men on the home front enabled them to expand their educational, economic, and professional activities and to assume leadership in their homes.

The early scholars of women's history showed a unique brand of courage in choosing to investigate new subjects and take new approaches to old ones. Often, like their subjects, they endured criticism and even ostracism by their academic colleagues. But their efforts have unquestionably been worthwhile, because with the publication of each new study and book another piece of the historical patchwork is sewn into place, revealing an increasingly comprehensive picture of the role of women in our rich and varied history.

Such books on groups of women are essential, but books that focus on the lives of individuals are equally indispensable. Biographies can be inspirational, offering their readers the example of people with vision who have looked outside themselves for their goals and have often struggled against great obstacles to achieve them. Marian Anderson, for instance, had to overcome racial bigotry in order to perfect her art and perform as a concert singer. Isadora Duncan defied the rules of classical dance to find true artistic freedom. Jane Addams had to break down society's notions of the proper role for women in order to create new social institutions, notably the settlement house. All of these women had to come to terms both with themselves and with the world in which they lived. Only then could they move ahead as pioneers in their chosen callings.

Biography can inspire not only by adulation but also by realism. It helps us to see not only the qualities in others that we hope to emulate but also, perhaps, the weaknesses that made them "human." By helping us identify with the subject on a more personal level they help us to feel that we, too, can achieve such goals. We read about Eleanor Roosevelt, for example, who occupied a unique and seemingly enviable position as the wife of the president. Yet we can sympathize with her inner dilemma: an inherently shy woman who had to force herself to live a most public life in order to use her position to benefit others. We may not be able to imagine ourselves having the immense poetic talent of Emily Dickinson, but from her story we can understand the challenges faced by a creative woman who was expected to fulfill many family responsibilities. And though few of us will ever reach the level of athletic accomplishment displayed by Wilma Rudolph or Babe Zaharias, we can still appreciate their spirit, their overwhelming will to excel.

A biography is a multifaceted lens. It is first of all a magnification, the intimate examination of one particular life. But at the same time, it is a wide-angle lens, informing us about the world in which the subject lived. We come away from reading about one life knowing more about the social, political, and economic fabric of the time. It is for this reason, perhaps, that the great New England essayist Ralph Waldo Emerson wrote, in 1841, "There is properly no history: only biography." And it is also why biography, and particularly women's biography, will continue to fascinate writers and readers alike.

Lillian Hellman

Lillian Hellman was 29 years old when the 1934 opening of her first staged play, The Children's Hour, *transformed her into a celebrated playwright.*

ONE

"The Children's Hour"

The 1934 Broadway opening of Lillian Hellman's first staged play, *The Children's Hour*, took theatergoers by storm and launched a career that spanned five decades. Her first solo dramatic effort, the play had not been easy for Hellman to write. When she embarked on the project she was an unsuccessful writer who earned her living as a script reader for Broadway producer and director Herman Shumlin. She had struggled for more than a year to complete the play, rewriting it some 14 times. Hellman's efforts had been overseen by her companion and mentor, mystery novelist Dashiell Hammett. It was Hammett who had suggested the idea for the play's plot, which was based on a 19th-century court case in which two headmistresses of a respected Scottish girls' boarding school were accused of immoral behavior by a vindictive student.

Unsure of the result of her labors, Hellman submitted her finished play to her boss, Herman Shumlin, without signing it. But even in her uncertainty the 29-year-old writer exhibited a glimmer of the brash confidence that would become part of her public image: She told Shumlin to pay special attention to the script, for it was the best she had read since she began working for him.

Set in a small Massachusetts town during the early 1930s, the play's action closely mirrors the events that led up to the British court case. In Hellman's fictionalized version, a young girl, Mary Tilford, falsely accuses the two headmistresses of her boarding school, Karen Wright and Martha Dobie, of lesbianism. Her charges are motivated by her dislike of the school and a desire to manipulate her grandmother, the wealthy and influential Amelia Tilford, into allowing her to leave.

Hellman worked as a script reader for producer and director Herman Shumlin (pictured) when she wrote The Children's Hour. *Impressed with her play, he agreed to stage it.*

Mary convinces her grandmother that her story is true, and the older woman hastens to warn the other pupils' parents, who immediately withdraw their daughters. The headmistresses' attempts to refute Mary's charge prove fruitless, for she has blackmailed one of her more timid schoolmates into supporting her lie. Although the teachers sue for libel, they lose their case. The one person who might have cleared them, Martha Dobie's aunt, Lily Mortar, has left the school and refuses to come to their aid out of fear of scandal.

The school is closed and the teachers become outcasts. The two women are devastated by the loss of their livelihoods and reputations, and Martha Dobie eventually commits suicide. Within minutes of this senseless death, Amelia Tilford arrives to apologize and offer compensation, for Mary's lie has been discovered. But by then it is too late, and Karen Wright rebuffs Tilford's overture.

Thematically, *The Children's Hour* raises a number of important issues that would resurface throughout Hellman's career. The play explores the destructive power of malicious lies and the cruelty with which society responds to those who seem to deviate from its norms. *The Children's Hour* also attacks the arrogance of the rich and powerful. Finally, in the refusal of Lily Mortar to come to the teachers' aid, Hellman presents a theme that she will return to again: Evil often triumphs because weak people are too fearful to rise against it.

Shumlin was impressed by *The Children's Hour* and pleased when he learned that it was the work of his young play reader. He agreed to stage the play but ran into trouble when he tried to assemble a cast. Hellman's was not the first play of the period to mention the subject of homosexuality, but the topic was still considered quite controversial in 1934, and many actors Shumlin approached turned down roles for fear that their careers would be ruined. These concerns were not ill founded: Only eight years earlier, the police had closed down *The Captive*, another play that dealt with homosexuality, and arrested its cast. But Shumlin was persistent and eventually found actors willing to gamble that *The Children's Hour* would not meet with a similar fate.

Anticipation—and apprehension—ran rampant in the weeks preceding the play's opening. "I'll never forget the tension and excitement of those rehearsals," recalled Eugenia Rawls, who played one of the students. "We all knew it was going to be something special." Theater owner Lee Shubert, who was financing the production, feared that the play might be *too* special. According to Hellman's memoir *Pentimento*, Shubert turned to her during rehearsals and grimly announced, "This play could land us all in jail." Hellman, who was eating her dinner, responded with typical irreverence: "I am eating a frankfurter and I don't want to think about jail. Would you like a piece of it?"

The Children's Hour, dedicated to Dashiell Hammett, opened in New York on the evening of November 20, 1934. Despite the cool manner in which Hellman had dismissed Lee Shubert's worries, she was far from confident about her first staged work. In an attempt to calm her nerves, she began drinking heavily before the curtain went up. As she confessed in *Pentimento*, her memory of that first night's performance was far from clear: "I think I saw the play from the back of the theatre, holding to the rail, but I am not sure: I do remember the final curtain and an audience yelling, 'Author,

author.' It was not all modesty that kept me from the curtain call—I couldn't have made backstage without falling." Hellman later regretted that her drinking bout had robbed her of her first sweet taste of success.

In the coming months *The Children's Hour* impressed critics and

Theater owner Lee Shubert is shown here in 1934, the same year that he financed The Children's Hour. *"This play," he told Hellman, "could land us all in jail."*

moved audiences. Some reviewers raised minor objections about the play's melodramatic plot devices, such as Martha's suicide and Mrs. Tilford's sudden change of heart. But most critics hailed the drama with enthusiastic praise. The public concurred, and *The Children's Hour* ran for 691 perfor-mances in New York, an unusually long run for a first play. At the end of its Broadway stint the production traveled across the United States and Europe for another year.

Controversy greeted the tour, however. Because of its provocative theme, *The Children's Hour* was censored in

Amelia Tilford confronts her granddaughter, Mary, in a scene from The Children's Hour. *The drama explored moral issues that concerned Hellman throughout her career.*

London, where it had to be performed at a private theater club; back in the United States it was banned in both Boston and Chicago. In the end, however, the uproar actually stimulated ticket sales as audiences flocked to see Hellman's "notorious" work.

One long-lasting consequence of the controversy over *The Children's Hour* involved the Pulitzer Prize for the best Broadway play of the 1934–35 season. Pulitzer Prizes—annual awards for achievement in journalism, literature, and other fields—have long been considered prestigious honors. In 1935 the Pulitzer committee bypassed Hellman's play even though it was the critical success of the season. Many observers felt that the committee's decision was an injustice motivated by the members' disapproval of Hellman's theme. This view was reinforced by the fact that 1935's drama award went to a more conventional work, *The Old Maid* by Zoe Akins. In awarding the prize to Akins, the committee had broken its own rule against giving the prize to any but original stories. It was common knowledge that Akins's play was an adaptation of a short story by Edith Wharton.

Responding to what they considered a blatant injustice, the drama critics of New York's major newspapers united to form a committee that came to be known as the New York Drama Critics Circle. Their goal was to present their own annual award for drama, one that would be based on more progressive standards than those of the Pulitzer committee. In the course of her career, Hellman would be the recipient of two of these prizes.

The opening of *The Children's Hour* had set the stage for Lillian Hellman's career. The play embodied the crisp writing and moral fervor that would mark most of her literary efforts. Furthermore, the heated public debate provoked by her drama foreshadowed the controversy that would surround Hellman for the rest of her professional life.

Lillian Hellman, shown here as a young woman, later remarked that her headstrong nature and overactive imagination made her "a prize nuisance child."

TWO

"A Prize Nuisance"

The only child of Max and Julia Hellman, Lillian Hellman was born in New Orleans, Louisiana, on June 20, 1905. She spent her first five years of life in the South, and was exposed to an important set of cultural influences during this period. Both of her parents provided the young girl with links to an exciting period in American history, an era when the country's population swelled with an influx of hopeful immigrants.

Lillian's maternal and paternal forebears were Jewish émigrés from Germany who had come to the United States during the large German-Jewish immigration of the mid-19th century. They came seeking greater economic opportunity, an escape from political turmoil, and an end to the religious persecution they had faced in their homeland. Because the United States was expanding geographically and eco-nomically during this period, condi-tions were ideal for many of the newcomers to carve out niches for themselves. German immigrants gen-erally encountered little discrimina-tion and found ample opportunities for earning a living. Unlike later waves of immigrants, many of these new arrivals did not remain on the East Coast but headed south and west, where they found work and established families.

Lillian Hellman's maternal great-grandfather, Isaac Marx, arrived in America in 1840 and made his way to Demopolis, Alabama. Starting out as a peddler, he quickly built his own dry goods business. By 1860, Isaac Marx and his family of 10 children had firmly established themselves in the middle class. Isaac's sons were even more suc-cessful, and the oldest, Jacob, became a prosperous banker. Sophie Marx, Ja-cob's younger sister and Lillian's grandmother, married Leonard Newhouse, a hardworking man who became a successful wholesale liquor dealer.

In contrast to Lillian's mother's family—and the industrious spirit of the era—her paternal grandparents were indifferent to both wealth and status. Bernard and Babette Hellman had emigrated from Germany to Louisiana in 1848. Bernard Hellman worked as a bookkeeper and served as a quartermaster in the Confederate army during the Civil War. Lillian Hellman later described her paternal grandparents as strong, loving people. She also noted that "they had, in a middle-class world, evidently been a strange couple, going their own way with little interest in money or position, loved and respected by their children."

Bernard and Babette Hellman gave their family legacies that would prove more valuable than the wealth of the Marxes and Newhouses. They instilled

Strollers examine street vendors' wares in early 20th-century New Orleans. Lillian Hellman was born in the Louisiana city in 1905.

Entering New York harbor, immigrants gaze hopefully at the Statue of Liberty. Hellman's relatives came from Germany in the mid-19th century, seeking a better way of life.

in their three children—Max, Hannah, and Jenny—a profound love of learning. They also encouraged their offspring to tolerate individual differences and show humanitarian concern for those less fortunate than they.

Julia Newhouse had some difficulty adjusting to the loving and offbeat environment she entered when she married Max Hellman and moved into the New Orleans boardinghouse run by his sisters, Jenny and Hannah. In her memoirs, Lillian Hellman characterized her mother as a "sweet eccentric" with a penchant for churches and charitable causes. Hannah and Jenny, whom Lillian Hellman described as "large women, funny and generous," did their best to shield their refined sister-in-law from some of their rougher boarders. In many ways the outspoken and lively young Lillian had more in common with her aunts than with her quiet mother, whom she came to appreciate only in her adult years.

Lillian and her parents lived at her aunts' boardinghouse until she reached the age of five, when her father and mother moved into their own home in New Orleans. In 1911 Max Hellman's shoe manufacturing business, which he had started with his wife's dowry, failed. Hoping to make a fresh start, he moved his family to New York City. The Hellmans rented an apartment on Manhattan's Upper West Side—close to Julia's wealthy Marx-Newhouse relatives, who had moved north a few years earlier. But this new proximity did not improve Max's relationship with his in-laws, who considered him a hopeless failure. Young Lillian perceived this attitude and was hurt that anyone could disapprove of her beloved father.

The move to New York marked the beginning of a phase of Lillian's life that lasted for the next decade, until she was 16 years old. As Max Hellman struggled to earn a living working for various companies, he continually moved his wife and daughter from one location to another. Eventually, the Hellmans spent six months of each year in New York and six months in New Orleans, where they lived in Jenny and Hannah's boardinghouse.

This was not a happy time for Lillian, for the early New York years were marked by genuine poverty. Hellman later recalled that her family was "shabby poor" until her father became a successful traveling salesman. In Lillian's eyes, the Hellmans' fragile financial situation was underscored by their weekly visits to her wealthy grandmother Sophie Newhouse's elegant Manhattan apartment. As she later related in her memoirs, Hellman was frightened by her grandmother, a "silent, powerful, severe woman." Sophie's brother, Jacob Marx, was equally intimidating, "a man of great force . . . who was given to breaking the spirit of people for the pleasure of the exercise." In *An Unfinished Woman*, Hellman described her bewilderment at the stiff formality observed at her grandmother's: "Heavy weather hung over the lovely oval rooms. True, there were parties for my aunts, but the parties, to a peeping child in the servants' hall, seemed so muted that I was long convinced that on fancy occasions grown people moved their lips without making sounds."

The topic of conversation at Marx-Newhouse family gatherings was invariably money: "who had the most money, or who spent it too lavishly, who would inherit what, which had bought what ring that would last forever, who what jewel she would best have been without." Hellman later acknowledged that these encounters, in which she and her parents were clearly deemed inferior because of their lack of money, had a lasting impact on her life: "[They] made me into an angry child and forever caused in me a wild extravagance mixed with respect for money and those who have it."

Max and Julia Hellman's financial problems became a source of conflict. As Lillian learned quite early, tensions between her parents were also caused by her father's repeated infidelities. After seeing him with another woman one day, Lillian threw herself out of a fig tree that had become a beloved

This 1912 photograph shows Riverside Drive, which runs along
Manhattan's Upper West Side. The Hellmans lived nearby when they
moved to New York in 1911.

Lillian attended Manhattan's Public School 6, shown here in 1920. Although she was a poor student, she loved to read on her own.

hideout during her family's visits to New Orleans. The fall broke her nose, and for the rest of her life Hellman would have a crooked profile to remind her of the incident.

Family problems were not the only source of conflict in Lillian Hellman's youth. School became a particular source of frustration, largely because her family's frequent moves between New York and New Orleans played havoc with her education. As she described her youth in *An Unfinished Woman*, she was unable to find a niche for herself in either the North or the South: "This constant need for adjustment in two very different worlds made formal education into a kind of frantic tennis game, sometimes played with children whose strokes had force and brilliance, sometimes with those who could barely hold the racket."

Predictably, Lillian's disorientation led to rebelliousness. At her Manhattan elementary school she developed a reputation among teachers and parents for being difficult. With her best friend, Helen Schiff, Lillian cut classes on whim, defied curfews, and smoked cigarettes. According to Hellman biographer William Wright, the scandalized school principal warned Mrs. Schiff that Lillian was "a bad influence on her daughter."

In New Orleans, on the other hand, Lillian simply avoided school: "I skipped school at least once a week and often twice, knowing that nobody cared or would report my absence." On those days, she would start out for school only to double back and take refuge in her fig-tree hideout. There she read avidly, "filled with the passions that can only come to the bookish."

Lillian's experiences in New Orleans fostered her love of reading and, eventually, writing. Her father's family encouraged her to read extensively. In later years she would fondly recall Saturday afternoon trips with her Aunt Hannah to New Orleans's celebrated French Quarter, where the two would buy "smelly old leather books." And early on, Lillian displayed a writer's fascination with other people's life stories. To satisfy this curiosity, she spent a great deal of time with her aunts' boarders. "I guess I was the only one who ever listened to the guests," she wrote in *An Unfinished Woman*, "and they talked to me for hours."

Lillian's active—some might say overactive—imagination led her into a series of misadventures. As Hellman told writer Margaret Harriman, she and her friend Helen Schiff became caught up in the intrigues of World War I. The United States was at war with Germany, and Lillian and Helen were constantly on the lookout for German spies. Spotting two "long-haired fellows" one afternoon, they reported the men to a police officer. Much to the girls' disappointment, these suspicious characters proved to be not spies but a musician and a professor. It seems likely that these men would have agreed with Hellman's later assessment: "I must have been a prize nuisance child."

At the age of 10 or 12, Hellman began to write stories and poems. When she entered high school in New York, she began experimenting with acting and journalism. While still the rebel (she is said to have cut classes some 23 times during her last 2 years at Manhattan's Wadleigh High School), Hellman wrote a column called "It Seems to Me, Jr." for the school newspaper. Her pieces were modeled on those of Heywood Broun, a popular liberal journalist of the period. She also had a small part as a villain in a school play entitled *Mrs. Gorringe's Necklace*. When a stage door jammed, barring her exit, she took advantage of the situation to try to steal the show with some ad-libbed lines.

As Lillian Hellman prepared for her high school graduation, her future was already taking shape. Her interests in

Journalist Heywood Broun impressed the young Hellman with his outspoken idealism. His column "It Seems to Me" inspired her to write a similar series for her high school newspaper.

Lillian Hellman graduated from Manhattan's Wadleigh High School, pictured here, in 1922. Her interest in the theater grew out of her involvement in school productions.

theater and literature would lead her to her life's work, and her personality already displayed the warmth, flamboyance, and combativeness that would stay with her for the rest of her life. As her friend and biographer Peter Feibleman would remark of her years later, "The biggest difference between Lillian as a grown-up and Lillian as a child was that she was taller."

Hellman studied at both New York University and Columbia University, but after two years she opted to leave school to pursue a career in publishing in 1924.

THREE

Starting Out

Lillian Hellman graduated from Wadleigh High School in May 1922, just a month before her 17th birthday. That fall she began attending classes at the newly opened Washington Square branch of New York University. This division of the university was then merely a floor of rooms in an office building in Greenwich Village. The more prestigious branch of New York University, located uptown, did not accept women at that time. Although Hellman also attended summer school at Columbia University, her response to college was unenthusiastic. She had hoped to attend Smith, the respected women's college in Northampton, Massachusetts, but her family's financial situation made it impossible for her to go away to school.

"I was, of course, not where I wanted to be," Hellman later wrote of her university days, "and I envied those of my friends who were." She developed a slapdash approach to her studies. It was not that she did not work, but she insisted on pursuing her studies in her own way. According to a former classmate, Hellman came up with a novel reason for copying from the student's test paper one day: "I know what *I* think about the plays; but for the test I have to know what the *instructor* thinks about them."

In 1924, deciding that she was simply "wasting time," Hellman dropped out of college. According to biographer William Wright, if she had not quit school, she might well have been expelled for poor grades. Hellman later described herself during this period as a "wild and headstrong girl . . . oversensitive, overdaring because I was shy and frightened."

29

Yet failure in college did not mean that Hellman lacked ambition. Thanks to a chance meeting at a party, she landed her first job in the autumn of 1924. She began working as an editorial assistant and manuscript reader at Boni and Liveright, then one of the country's newest and most progressive publishing houses. Established in 1917, Liveright's had quickly developed a reputation for publishing the most gifted and original writers on the American scene. Novelists William Faulkner and Ernest Hemingway, poets T. S. Eliot and e. e. cummings, and playwright Eugene O'Neill were just a few of the notable authors published there.

Hellman began working during the Roaring Twenties, an era of rebellion, frivolity, and relaxed social standards. Boni and Liveright reflected the spirit of the times. Office procedures were

Today New York University has an extensive campus surrounding Washington Square Park, shown here in 1920. When Hellman studied there, NYU's downtown branch was just a few classrooms.

informal, work hours were generally set by the staff, and many employees napped at their desks—often to recuperate from Liveright's uninhibited company parties. The 19-year-old Hellman, well liked by her co-workers for her keen intelligence and sharp-tongued wit, was a welcome addition to these affairs. Unaware that she would soon join their ranks, Hellman mingled with some of the leading literary figures of the day.

Lillian Hellman remained at Boni and Liveright for more than a year. She recommended a number of books that were good but not necessarily marketable, and in general her work record left much to be desired. During one of Liveright's periodic "efficiency clean-ups," Hellman heard that there was talk of firing her: "I had misplaced an important manuscript, I didn't know how to file, my typing was erratic, my manuscript reports were severe." She later acknowledged that she would have been fired at the time had word not gotten around that she was pregnant. According to Hellman biographer Carl Rollyson, this news "provoked the sympathetic interest of every member in the firm. Suddenly she was a 'showcase,' the object of advice and curiosity. The men expected her to break down, name the child's father, and enact the role of helpless female. Instead, she withdrew from them in anger, refusing to talk or to be sent home—even after an abortion." Abortion was against the law at that time, so Hellman had to find someone willing to perform the operation in secret. She was more for-

Horace Liveright, above, was Hellman's employer at Boni and Liveright. Hellman read manuscripts and did clerical work at the prestigious book publishing house.

tunate than many women undergoing illegal abortions: She found a certified doctor to perform the surgery and suffered few complications afterward.

On December 31, 1925, 6 months after her abortion, the 20-year-old Hellman married her longtime boyfriend, Arthur Kober. He was short, stocky, and handsome, and like Hellman, he wanted to be a professional writer. Born in Austria-Hungary in 1900, Kober had immigrated to the United States with his family when he was four years old. When Hellman met Kober he was an

Young women participate in a 1926 dance contest. Hellman came of age during the "Roaring Twenties," a time of youthful frivolity and liberal morality.

energetic and industrious young man who had worked his way from department store stock boy to Broadway press agent. He was also a struggling playwright whose first staged effort closed a week before the couple's wedding. Kober would eventually make his mark as the author of some 30 screenplays and the Broadway hits *Having a Wonderful Time* and *Wish You Were Here.* As one of her friends commented at the time, Hellman was attracted by Kober's talent: "She always said he had a great future, and I think that meant a great deal to her—to be associated with someone who had a future."

Hellman left Boni and Liveright to marry Kober, but her desire to work reasserted itself shortly after their honeymoon. She began visiting Liveright's again but was afraid to ask for her old job back because of both her past work record and her suspicion that the company's fortunes were declining. Through Kober, she eventually got a job as a publicity agent for a Broadway revue called *Bunk of 1926.* The show opened in February 1926 and closed soon afterward. This job had, however, given Hellman her first professional involvement with the theater.

Hellman's next position was as an

occasional book reviewer for the *New York Herald Tribune*, where she earned less than five dollars a review. These pieces were generally astute and eloquent, and their publication marked the first time her name appeared in print. Hellman was also writing fiction during this period, but she invariably found her work unsatisfactory and discarded it.

In late 1926 Kober was offered the opportunity to go to France as editor of a new literary magazine, the *Paris Comet*, which was aimed at Americans living abroad. Kober accepted the post, and in early 1927 he and Hellman moved into a small hotel on Paris's Left Bank, an area famous for its artistic and intellectual activities. They spent much of their time sightseeing, eating in inexpensive restaurants, and socializing with other young Americans. Hellman reworked several of her short stories, and these were published in the *Paris Comet*. She later dismissed these pieces as "lady writer" stories—"the kind where the man puts down his fork and the woman knows it's over."

Hellman and Kober returned to America in mid-1927, and the couple moved into a house in Douglaston, Long Island. Kober worked as a press agent for the hit Broadway play *Green Pastures*; Hellman spent most of her days reading, playing bridge, and experimenting with southern cooking. Between June and December she also contributed four book reviews to the *Herald Tribune*, among them a very positive review of William Faulkner's novel *Mosquitoes*, which she described as having a "brilliance that you can rightfully expect only in the writings of a few."

The 22-year-old Hellman became increasingly frustrated with the aimlessness of her life. Although she enjoyed domestic tasks such as cooking, it was clear that she was not cut out to be a traditional wife. Thanks to her husband's encouragement and contacts, she got a job reading plays for Anne Nichols, one of the few successful female playwrights of the period. But Nichols's attempts at producing plays failed. When her company folded, Kober found Hellman brief assign-

Hellman married Arthur Kober, pictured here, on December 31, 1925. The couple had a great deal in common and remained friends even after their 1932 divorce.

ments as a play reader for a number of other producers.

In the winter of 1928 Hellman accepted a job that Kober himself had rejected. For four months, while her husband remained in Manhattan, she worked as a publicity agent for a stock theater company in Rochester, New York. She did very little writing during this period. Hellman later wrote she had "convinced myself that I was not meant to be a writer."

The following summer she treated herself to a vacation in Europe. After visiting several countries Hellman settled in Bonn, Germany, where she considered enrolling at the local university. Her plans abruptly changed after a frightening brush with Adolf Hitler's emerging Nazi party.

Hellman had been invited to join a student group that she took to be a socialist organization. When some of the group leaders asked her if she had

Patrons crowd the sidewalk tables at a Paris café in 1927, the year that Hellman and Kober lived in the French capital.

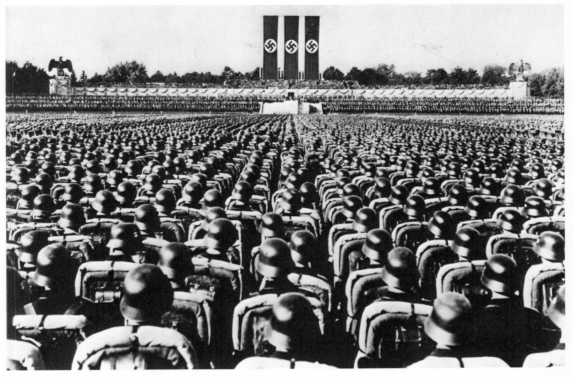

A sea of German troops listens to an address by Nazi leader Adolf Hitler. Hellman had a brush with the emerging Nazi party during a 1929 visit to Bonn, Germany.

any Jewish relatives, she discovered that she had made a tremendous mistake: The organization she had nearly joined was a wing of Hitler's National Socialist German Workers' (Nazi) party. Repelled by her first encounter with nazism, she left Germany the next day and returned to the United States. Her experience would contribute to her passionate opposition to Hitler's regime when he came to power in the 1930s. On a more personal level, Hellman remarked in her memoir *Scoundrel Time* that her experience in Bonn marked "the first time in my life I thought about being a Jew."

In 1930 Lillian Hellman moved to Hollywood, California, where her husband had been hired as a screenwriter. In the coming years Hellman would herself write several film scripts.

FOUR

The Making of a Playwright

In February 1930, several months after Hellman's return from Europe, Arthur Kober took a job as a Hollywood screenwriter. His salary was an impressive $450 a week, "more money than we'd ever seen," Hellman later wrote. Kober left for Hollywood, but Hellman, who was not eager to move west, procrastinated for several months before joining her husband.

Kober's windfall came at a time when many Americans were experiencing financial hard times. The stock market crash of 1929 had signaled the beginning of the most severe economic crisis that the country had ever known, the period later called the Great Depression. Lasting roughly from 1929 through the early 1940s, the depression affected people of all classes. During its worst phase it resulted in the failure of thousands of banks and businesses, sent millions of farmers into bankruptcy,

and imposed massive unemployment and poverty upon untold numbers of men and women who had formerly been self-sufficient. For hundreds of others, the hardship of that period ended in literal starvation and even death. Large-scale federal intervention, such as government-sponsored work programs, alleviated the crisis, but the U.S. economy did not fully recover until the country began gearing up for World War II.

Just as the Great Depression began, the American movie industry entered an unprecedented phase of growth. In 1927, two years before the stock market crash, Warner Brothers Studio introduced Hollywood's first talking movie, *The Jazz Singer*, starring Al Jolson. The innovation was so successful that attendance at movie theaters nearly doubled in two years. The invention of "talkies" contributed to Holly-

Unemployed men eat at a charity kitchen during the Great Depression. This period of worldwide economic decline began with the stock market crash of 1929.

wood's survival during the early years of the depression. Another reason the film industry thrived during this period is that many Americans turned to movies as a means of forgetting their hard lives, for a few hours at least.

Hollywood guaranteed a livelihood to scores of writers, for film companies constantly sought talented men and women to fill the demand for intriguing plots and credible dialogue. The studios' searches often ended in New York, which had become a repository of first-rate talent, thanks to Broadway and the publishing industry. Among the many respected eastern writers commandeered by Hollywood at the time were F. Scott Fitzgerald, Nathanael West, and William Faulkner. While Arthur Kober was not then a "name" writer, he was among the many New Yorkers who moved to Hollywood in response to the movie industry's demand, thereby avoiding the worst ravages of the Great Depression.

During her first months in California, Hellman spent her days reading, sunbathing, and socializing. In the evenings she and her husband joined in Hollywood's lively and uninhibited nightlife. Hellman was equally at ease dining at the select Clover Club as at an informal card game with friends. But as much as she enjoyed socializing, she eventually grew restless with her aimless life.

Hellman then began working as a script reader at Metro-Goldwyn-Mayer (MGM) at a salary of $50 a week. Her job entailed writing concise summaries of material that might make for good film scripts. The sources from which she and the other readers worked covered the spectrum from magazine articles to full-length novels. Hellman quickly came to dislike her job, for the hours were long and the work mechanical. When she attempted to organize her fellow readers to fight for better working conditions, she was branded a troublemaker and eventually fired. Despite her discontent, as her biographer Carl Rollyson pointed out, Hellman's stint as a script reader was an invaluable learning experience for her, for it taught her to write effective screenplays. In a very few years this skill would enable her to write complete movie scripts on her own, something that many professional writers, among

them F. Scott Fitzgerald and William Faulkner, were never able to do.

Lillian Hellman's personal and professional life were forever changed after she met author Dashiell Hammett at a

Al Jolson wears "blackface" in the first talking movie, 1927's The Jazz Singer. *In an era of widespread prejudice, whites often played black roles, emphasizing racial stereotypes.*

Hollywood gathering in the fall of 1930. At the time of their meeting Hammett was a 36-year-old writer of detective fiction whose most recent novel, *The Maltese Falcon*, had taken the literary world by storm. Hammett's book would profoundly influence mystery writers around the world, and its "tough guy" hero, private detective Sam Spade, would be immortalized in the classic John Huston film starring Humphrey Bogart.

Hammett was born in 1894 into an old but poor Maryland family. In order to supplement his family's income, he left school at the age of 13 and began working as a laborer. At 20 he worked briefly as a clerk and apprentice "operative" for the Pinkerton Detective Agency. He entered the army during

A studio employee analyzes a screenplay. Hellman briefly worked as a script reader for Metro-Goldwyn-Mayer, but was fired after she agitated for better working conditions.

World War I, but was discharged after he contracted tuberculosis. Over the next several years Hammett was often hospitalized for his illness, which left him with the fatalistic belief that he did not have long to live. Nevertheless, during one of his hospital stays, he met and fell in love with a pretty young nurse, Josephine Dolan. In 1921, he and Dolan were married; in 1937, after two children and numerous separations, they were divorced.

In spite of his health problems Hammett continued to work at various jobs and to pursue his passion for writing. During the 1920s he sold a number of stories to detective-fiction magazines. Hammett's first two novels, *Red Harvest* and *The Dain Curse*, were both published in 1929 to good reviews. But it was *The Maltese Falcon* that brought him recognition and wealth. Although he would live until 1961, Hammett wrote only two novels after 1930: *The Glass Key*, published in 1931, and 1934's *The Thin Man*. In the course of his brief literary career, he almost single-handedly revolutionized the detective novel. He infused his gritty tales of theft, blackmail, and murder with vivid, hard-boiled poetry. And he established the tradition of the tough, authentically American private detective who—in contrast to the more cerebral approach of a Sherlock Holmes—is not afraid to use physical force when confronted with a violent world.

When Hellman met Hammett in 1930, he was a tall, handsome, worldly man, separated from his wife and children and at the peak of his career.

Hellman called mystery writer Dashiell Hammett "the handsomest sight" she had ever seen. The two began a 30-year relationship in 1930.

A gangster confronts Nick and Nora Charles in the film version of Hammett's novel The Thin Man. *The irreverent Charleses were partly modeled on Hellman and Hammett.*

According to Hammett biographer Diane Johnson, Hammett found the 25-year-old Hellman an amusing and ambitious young woman, "little and lively and tough as nails." As he got to know Hellman, Hammett also thought that she had the potential to be a successful writer, provided she conquered her laziness and insecurity. For her part, Hellman was attracted by Hammett's good looks, intelligence, and literary success.

Hellman began seeing Hammett openly, with her husband's full knowledge and tolerance. Kober seems to have loved Hellman a great deal, but he knew that any attempt to control his strong-willed wife would only backfire. As he confided to a friend, he hoped that Hellman's attraction to Hammett would soon wane. But this did not happen, and in 1932 Hellman and Kober divorced. Nevertheless, they remained close and supportive friends until Kober's death in 1975.

Hellman and Hammett moved to New York, where they lived in a succession of Manhattan hotels. They continued the kind of barhopping that they had enjoyed in Hollywood, from the then famous Small's Paradise in Harlem to journalists' gathering places in midtown Manhattan. Their dizzying social life, which revolved around unexpected guests and spontaneous parties, eventually found its way into Hammett's last novel, *The Thin Man*. Aspects of their conversations and personalities also helped shape the exchanges between the novel's protagonists, Nick and Nora Charles.

As Hammett's companion, Hellman attended an array of literary parties and met many of the era's most celebrated writers. Novelist William Faulkner, whom Hellman had praised in one of her early book reviews, became a particular friend. He, Hammett, and Hellman would often spend entire evenings discussing literature. In the morning, Hellman might well awaken to discover Faulkner still there, asleep in the living room. Through Hammett, Hellman also met writer and wit Dorothy Parker, who would become a lifelong friend.

Although she still considered herself an aspiring novelist and short story writer, Hellman briefly experimented with writing plays in 1932. Collaborating with Louis Kronenberger, an old friend from her days at Boni and Liveright, she penned *Dear Queen*, a social satire set in the 18th century. Hellman and Kronenberger sent the play to producers all over New York. But none accepted it, and the play never reached the stage.

Hellman was more successful with a pair of short stories she wrote soon afterward. She set to work with both Hammett's encouragement and the knowledge that her manuscripts would be given serious consideration by his literary contacts. Instead of the restrained "lady-like" stories she had written before, she began to experiment with humor. In 1933 and 1934 "I Call Her Mama Now" and "Perberty in Los Angeles" were published in the *American Spectator*. Both stories satirized the attempts of parents to force modernity on their adolescent children. Their publication brought Hellman a measure of success as a short story writer, but her career soon took a different course.

Parties had often been lucky meeting places for Hellman: She landed her first job through a chance encounter at a party in 1924; six years later she met Dashiell Hammett at a Hollywood gathering. This pattern repeated itself at a 1933 gala hosted by composer Ira Gershwin. It was there that Hellman attracted the attention of Herman Shumlin, the man who, after Hammett, would most influence her career as a playwright. Shumlin was one of Broadway's finest directors and producers, renowned for staging plays that were serious, financially successful,

Writer and wit Dorothy Parker, shown here, was one of the literary figures Hellman met through Dashiell Hammett. The two women became lifelong friends.

Hellman's career as a playwright began with the 1934 Broadway production of The Children's Hour. *She would produce several more hits in the coming decades.*

and of high artistic quality. Impressed by Hellman, he offered her a job as a play reader, and she readily accepted.

Hellman's eagerness to work for Shumlin was motivated more by disorder in her home life than by career ambitions. She was not yet self-supporting, and although Hammett earned a good deal of money from his books and film scripts, his drinking binges and financial carelessness often left them deeply in debt. He and Hellman were periodically forced to flee from one hotel to another because they were unable to pay their bills. The couple's most recent address had been

the Sutton Hotel on East 56th Street. The hotel's night manager, author Nathanael West, often lent empty rooms to fellow writers either without charge or at very low rates. But Hellman was not content to rely on West's charity, and she hoped that her play-reading job would bring a measure of economic stability.

While she read the plays of others Hellman began to think about writing one of her own. Her plot idea came from a story that Hammett had discovered in *Bad Companions*, William Roughead's book on notable British court cases. The account that fascinated Hammett was called "Closed Doors, or the Great Drumsheugh Case." It involved two headmistresses of a respected girls' school who were falsely accused of lesbianism by a student. The teachers sued for libel, and after a 10-year struggle, they were cleared by the House of Lords. But by that time both their careers and their personal lives had been destroyed. Hammett, who had just finished *The Thin Man*, thought that the account would make a good play. He toyed with the idea of writing it himself before he suggested that Hellman take on the job.

Hellman mulled the idea over during the spring and summer of 1933. She had taken a leave of absence from her work to enjoy an extended vacation with Hammett in the Florida Keys. When they returned to New York, Hellman began working seriously on her play. Hammett read her many drafts, making suggestions and offering criticism. He was often an invaluable help to Hellman, but he could also be a hindrance: His drinking and socializing distracted her from her work. In the summer of 1934 she went to Paris alone in order to finish her play.

Hellman completed *The Children's Hour* and presented it to Herman Shumlin. Events moved quickly from that point. The play went into production in October and opened to wide acclaim a month later. As that opening night drew to a close, Lillian Hellman took her first step into American theatrical history.

*Thirty-year-old Lillian Hellman arrives in Hollywood in 1935 to begin
a lucrative stint as a screenwriter for MGM studios.*

FIVE

Joining Crusades

The commercial and critical success of *The Children's Hour* had a number of consequences for Lillian Hellman. Long accustomed to a precarious financial existence, she was now economically comfortable. She had also moved from relative obscurity to international renown. Her triumph in the New York theater also landed her an assignment to write film scripts for producer Sam Goldwyn of MGM—at the impressive salary of $2,500 a week. In 1931 she had been fired from a $50-a-week job as a studio manuscript reader. With her triumphant return to Hollywood four years later she joined the exclusive group of successful eastern writers then employed in the movie industry, and her salary was among the highest at the time.

Hellman and Hammett—who was also working as a screenwriter—rented a home together and got down to business. For her first script, Hellman collaborated with British playwright Mordaunt Shairp on a love story called *Dark Angel*. The film was released in 1935 and was well received at the box office. At its completion, Hellman's contract with MGM was renewed, and she was given complete freedom in choosing the subject of her next screenplay. She suggested that Goldwyn buy the rights to *The Children's Hour* so that she could adapt it for film. Goldwyn was warned against buying the play because it concerned lesbianism. But the studio chief—well known for his confused but often hilarious "Goldwynisms"—dismissed this idea. Perhaps confusing "lesbian" with "Lebanese," he reportedly replied: "That's all right . . . we'll make them Americans."

But while Goldwyn seemed oblivious to the controversy that would greet a film dealing with homosexuality, Hellman was aware that even passing mention of the topic would not get past the censors who screened every Hollywood production during that period. Accordingly, she replaced the homosexual theme with a heterosexual love triangle in the screen adaptation of her play. Entitled *These Three*, the film was directed by William Wyler and starred Merle Oberon, Miriam Hopkins, and Joel McCrea. When it was released in March 1936, *These Three* was both a critical and financial success.

Although Hellman's career was moving smoothly, her personal life was far from tranquil. Julia Hellman had died while her daughter was visiting New York for Thanksgiving in 1935. As Hellman later wrote in her memoirs, she did not realize how much she loved her mother until after she died. Hellman returned to the West Coast but found little solace there. Hammett's drinking had become uncontrollable. When sober, he was a gentle, even shy man. But when drunk, he became aggressive, particularly toward women. Hellman did her best to convince him to stop drinking, but her attempts proved futile. Although she insisted that he never abused her physically, some of her acquaintances, noticing occasional bruises and black eyes, thought otherwise.

Hellman's sorrow over her mother's death and her difficulties with Hammett took a high emotional toll and began to interfere with her work. Seeking a change of scene, she left Hammett in Hollywood and returned to New York in 1936. She rented an apartment in Greenwich Village, hosted a number of parties, and became romantically involved with Ralph Ingersoll, then managing editor of *Fortune* magazine. Her relationship with Hammett, however, was far from over, and she was soon commuting between New York and Hollywood. But from this point on she began to lead a more independent life.

Despite her affluence, Hellman became deeply interested in the economic crisis gripping the United States and much of the world. The deepening depression inspired political agitation and labor unrest across the nation. Even Hollywood was not immune. The movie industry had prospered during the early phases of the Great Depression, but in 1933 screenwriters were asked to take wage cuts to keep the studios from closing down. By 1935, the year Hellman won her lucrative contract with MGM, the overwhelming majority of screenwriters earned less then $10,000 a year. In addition, most had no job security between writing assignments and no control over whether or not they would be given credit for their work.

The writers responded by forming the Screen Writers Guild in 1933. Two years later the union still found it difficult to recruit new members, for open affiliation with the guild could jeopardize a writer's career. Additionally, many screenwriters were successful in other areas, such as book publishing and the theater. These fortunate individuals tended to be satisfied with their situations and unlikely to agitate for change.

Hellman was a successful young Broadway playwright who did not depend on films for her living. Nevertheless, she quickly joined the Screen Writers Guild and became actively in-

volved in its efforts to build a strong union and to recruit new members. During guild strategy sessions she passionately castigated her more restrained colleagues for their cautious dealings with the studios. According to her friend and fellow guild member Albert Hackett, Hellman's approach tended to be both militant and emotional: "She was somebody wonderful

Joel McCrea, Merle Oberon, and Miriam Hopkins appear in a scene from These Three, *Hellman's screen adaptation of* The Children's Hour.

Workers protest outside an automobile plant in Detroit, Michigan. Hellman's unsuccessful second play, Days to Come, *focused on the labor unrest that gripped the country in the 1930s.*

to have on your side, but then you were afraid she'd go too far."

Hellman's growing social awareness was also reflected in her second play, *Days to Come,* which she had completed in between guild activities and film commitments. The play's action centers around the labor-management struggle in a small midwestern town during the 1930s. The workers at the town's brush factory have gone on

strike against their well-meaning but desperate employer, who has been forced to cut their wages below the poverty level in an attempt to save his faltering business. The employer ultimately brings in strikebreakers in an attempt to force the laborers back to work. When one of these strikebreakers is murdered by a cohort in a drunken brawl, the murder is blamed on a union organizer, thereby providing a rationale for the strikebreakers to attack the workers. In the violence that ensues, the town is torn apart, the workers are worn down, and the strike finally ends.

Days to Come premiered at Broadway's Vanderbilt Theater on December 15, 1936. Despite its timely social and political relevance, the play was a flop. In her memoir *Pentimento*, Hellman described the play's catastrophic opening night:

> The carefully rehearsed light cues worked as if they were meant for another play; the props, not too complicated, showed up where nobody had ever seen them before and broke, or didn't break, with the malice of animated beings; good actors knew by the first twenty minutes they had lost the audience and thus became bad actors; the audience, maybe friendly as it came in, was soon restless and uncomfortable. The air of a theater is unmistakable: things go well or they do not. They did not.

Days to Come was badly received by reviewers and audiences alike. The critical consensus was that Hellman had overloaded the play, for in addition to its major theme of labor unrest, she also attempted to explore the personal lives of her characters and to develop a love relationship between two of them. Most critics agreed that she had simply given *Days to Come* too many characters, themes, and events. The play closed after only six performances.

Hellman was devastated by the failure of *Days to Come*. She began to fear that the success of her first play had been a mere fluke. "The failure of a second work," she confessed in *Penti-*

General Francisco Franco reviews his troops in 1936, the year he staged a coup against Spain's elected government. The fascist leader's bid for power led to the Spanish civil war.

51

Volunteers, such as those shown here, came from around the world to defend the embattled Spanish Republic. Hellman supported these antifascist forces, who were defeated in 1939.

mento, "is more damaging to a writer than failure ever will be again. It is then that the success of the first work seems an accident."

Her attention was soon diverted from her personal crisis by political events. In July 1936 Spanish army general Francisco Franco and a group of officers had led a coup against Spain's democratically elected government, initiating the Spanish civil war. Franco's efforts were supported by the leaders of Germany and Italy, both of whom had recently come to power after unseating democratic regimes. Both Hitler in Germany and Mussolini in Italy headed fascist (extreme right-wing) dictatorships. They now hoped to assist Franco in establishing a similar regime in Spain. As the Spanish republic was assailed by a would-be dictator, the democratic West maintained a "hands off" policy. Only the Soviet Union actively supported the established government in Spain by sending in weapons and advisers.

Although their governments remained silent, thousands of individuals throughout the world signed on to defend the Spanish republic. Forming volunteer units called International Brigades, they poured into the country to fight Franco's armies, and many lost their lives on Spanish soil. Hellman admired these brave men and women, and gave speeches and wrote articles in support of their cause.

In early 1937, at the invitation of poet and playwright Archibald MacLeish, Hellman flew to Paris to work on a documentary about the Spanish civil war. Among the other artists involved in the project were Dutch film director Joris Ivens and American novelists Ernest Hemingway and John Dos Passos. The film was intended to sway public opinion and raise money for democratic Spain. Hellman was enthusiastic about the project but was forced to fly back to New York after she came down with pneumonia. Although illness prevented her from taking part in the actual writing of the film's screenplay, she was credited with the original story idea.

Following a brief stay in the hospital Hellman was back on her feet and actively raising money for the documentary on Spain. Along with Archibald MacLeish and Dorothy Parker, she formed a corporation to help finance the film. The company was called Contemporary Historians, and she, Hammett, and a number of their friends each contributed $500. In April 1937 the film, entitled *The Spanish Earth*, was completed. Narrated by Ernest Hemingway, it is respected today as one of the earliest antifascist documentaries.

As *The Spanish Earth* neared completion, Hellman flew from New York to Hollywood to begin work on her third screenplay for MGM—and her second with acclaimed director William Wyler. Adapted from a 1935 play by Sidney Kingsley, *Dead End* effectively dramatized slum children's struggle for survival in a world controlled by criminals and wealthy opportunists. This exposé of life during the Great Depression starred actors Sylvia Sydney, Joel

McCrea, and Humphrey Bogart. Critical response to the film was good, and Hellman's involvement with it—as with *The Spanish Earth*—suggested the direction that her social and political consciousness was taking at the time.

On August 25, 1937, the day after *Dead End*'s opening at New York's Rivoli Theatre, Hellman sailed for Europe aboard the *Normandie*. Also on board were Dorothy Parker and her husband, Alan Campbell. Hellman

Actors portray slum youths in the film Dead End. *Hellman wrote the screenplay for this 1937 exposé of urban life during the Great Depression.*

spent several relaxing weeks with the couple in Paris before going on to the Soviet Union, where she had been invited to attend the Moscow Theater Festival.

In recent years Hellman had been increasingly attracted by the ideals that underlay communist philosophy. In the mid-1930s communism, with its promise of a classless, egalitarian society, seemed to many to be a viable solution to the difficult problems that faced democratic nations: the economic devastation of the Great Depression and the international threat of fascism. Hellman's growing sympathy toward communism was fostered by Hammett—a committed follower of communist philosopher Karl Marx—and by the Soviet Union's support of the antifascist forces in Spain.

Hellman later wrote that she did not realize that her trip to the Soviet Union brought her there during one of the most brutally repressive periods in the nation's history: the era of the Moscow show trials. To consolidate his power, Soviet leader Joseph Stalin was having scores of public officials and army officers placed on trial and executed for treason. Guilt or innocence was not the issue at these trials. Stalin was simply eradicating those who might prevent him from seizing absolute control of the state. During this same period he also instigated a series of purges that led to the execution of millions of Russians, from peasants and Communist party members to military officers and intellectuals. Hellman attributed her ignorance of these atrocities to her

Hellman boards the S.S. Normandie, *the cruise ship that took her to Europe for an extended tour in 1937. She visited several countries, including Spain and the Soviet Union.*

hosts, who limited her itinerary and prevented her from meeting with many Soviets. She also later commented that the American diplomats and journalists she socialized with "talked such gobbledygook . . . that one couldn't pick the true charges from the wild hatred."

A partial explanation for Hellman's refusal to believe the accusations against Stalin is revealed in *Pentimento*, a memoir she wrote years later. She admitted that her political views, born of idealism, could degenerate into blind stubbornness: "I am, in fact, bewildered by all injustice, at first certain that it cannot be, then shocked into rigidity, then finally as certain as a Grand Inquisitor that God wishes me to move ahead, correct and holy." In the case of the USSR, she was apparently so moved by Soviet ideals of economic and personal equality that she blinded herself to the actions of those such as Stalin, who committed hideous crimes while paying lip service to lofty goals.

The Spanish civil war was still raging during Hellman's visit to the USSR, and in October 1937 she traveled from Moscow to Spain to observe events at first hand. She stayed a few weeks, witnessing the physical hardships caused by the war. Writing about her experience in *An Unfinished Woman*, she described how touched she was by the sacrifices of those who were fighting an increasingly hopeless battle:

> . . . this war was like no other. Men had come great distances to fight here and when the war was over, if they came out alive, or with enough arms or legs or eyes to seem alive, there would be no world for them and no reward. They seemed to me noble people. Because I had never used that word before, it came hard to say it to myself even in the dark, and, as if I had had a vision of what I had missed in the world, I began to cry.

Years later, Hellman credited her experience in Spain with triggering her move from political liberal to radical. The pivotal moment, she wrote in her memoirs, came during a dinner party she attended in London after arriving from Spain that same day. The callous indifference of the guests crystallized her activism: "I suddenly was in the kind of rampage anger that I have known all my life, still know, and certainly in those days was not able, perhaps did not wish, to control." Hellman left the table so abruptly she upset her chair, and she stormed out of her host's house without a word of explanation.

Back in the United States Hellman became even more actively involved in activities on behalf of the Spanish republic, which, to her great sorrow, succumbed to Franco's forces in 1939. She was equally active in a number of leftist organizations—many of which were associated with the Communist party. On April 28, 1938, her name appeared alongside those of 149 other artists and intellectuals in an advertisement defending the verdicts reached at the Moscow show trials. Hellman's association with communist causes bred rumors that she was a party member, but she sidestepped these charges in her memoirs. However, after sifting through the evidence, many of her biographers have concluded that she was indeed a party member, at least from 1938 to 1940.

Whether or not she actually joined the Communist party, Hellman was a supporter of the Soviet Union for years, despite mounting evidence that the

Hellman meets with writer Vincent Sheean to discuss a project to raise funds for refugees. The playwright championed many political causes.

Lillian Hellman (far right) goes over the script of her latest play, The Little Foxes, *with cast members and director Herman Shumlin (left).*

USSR no longer adhered to the ideals that had inspired its 1917 revolution. But while many of her fellow radicals abandoned the party as abuses came to light, Hellman remained a staunch defender of the Soviet state.

For Lillian Hellman, 1938 did not simply signal the crystallization of her political orientation; it was also an important year for her career. After returning from Europe she began extensive research for her third—and to many, her best—play, *The Little Foxes*. She later remarked that *The Little Foxes* was the play she found most difficult to write, both because of the failure of *Days to Come* and because it was inspired by memories of her mother's family, the Marxes and the Newhouses. The play was set in the Deep South in 1900, and Hellman took great care in ensuring the play's historical accuracy. She did extensive research, filling two notebooks with information about southern history, economics, and culture. She was equally conscientious when writing the play, revising it some eight or nine times.

Hellman's progress was interrupted in May 1938 when Hammett, then in Hollywood, suffered a nervous breakdown. He was smuggled out of his hotel—where he owed an $8,000 bill—and flown to New York. Hellman met him at the airport with an ambulance and escorted him to a hospital. She visited him there often, and after nearly a month his condition seemed to improve. She went back to her play, in which the recovering Hammett took a great interest.

The Little Foxes centers around the power struggles within a wealthy southern clan. The members of the Hubbard family are so driven by selfishness and greed that they habitually manipulate and exploit one another for power and economic gain. Their obsession leads to theft, blackmail, and at the play's climax, murder. The play's moral is summed up in one of the character's lines: "Well, there are people who eat the earth and eat all the people on it . . . and other people who stand around and watch them do it." This theme—that inactivity in the face of evil can be as dangerous as evil itself—shaped Hellman's political views and would inspire several other plays.

As *The Little Foxes* went into production, the casting of the iron-willed main character, Regina Hubbard, became a problem. As Hellman wrote the part, Regina was a mesmerizing schemer, and many leading actresses rejected the part as being too "unsympathetic." Eventually, despite Hellman's reservations about her relative youth and reputation for offstage exhibitionism, southerner Tallulah Bankhead was cast in the part.

After successful out-of-town tryouts in Baltimore, *The Little Foxes* opened at New York's National Theater on February 15, 1939. The play received unrestrained critical praise and ran for 410 performances before beginning its national tour. Critic and author Robert Benchley called it "awfully, awfully good," and *Life* magazine dubbed it "the year's strongest play." Today *The Little Foxes* is considered an American classic. In 1941 it was made into a powerful motion picture written by Hellman, directed by William Wyler, and starring Bette Davis. Eight years later the play became the basis of a Marc Blitzstein opera, *Regina*, which in 1967 had a highly successful revival at Lincoln Center in New York City.

With the money she earned from *The Little Foxes*, Hellman made the first significant investment of her life. In June 1939 she purchased Hardscrabble Farm, a sprawling 130-acre estate in Westchester County, New York. For the next 12 years, until its forced sale

Tallulah Bankhead (left) appears in a scene from The Little Foxes.
Many critics consider this saga of greed and moral deterioration
Hellman's finest work.

in 1951, Hardscrabble's lake and woods provided Hellman with an alternative to the pressures of her public life. The farm was also the first real home that she had known in her adult years; she went there both to enjoy solitude and to entertain. Although she and Hammett continued to maintain separate residences in New York City, Hard-scrabble quickly became as much of a home to him as it was to her.

But Lillian Hellman's hideaway would not shield her from the international developments that were transforming the world during this period. In the coming years, these events would have a profound impact on both her life and her work.

Lillian Hellman's plays and screenplays of the 1940s served to express her political convictions, particularly her horror at the spread of fascism across Europe.

SIX

Politics and Art

As *The Little Foxes* settled into a long Broadway run, events were unfolding in the international arena that would shortly signal the outbreak of widespread conflict. To the embarrassment and confusion of Soviet sympathizers such as Hellman, in August 1939 the USSR signed a nonaggression pact with Nazi Germany. A month later the two nations invaded Poland, ushering in World War II. In late 1939 and early 1940 the Soviet Union successfully conquered its northern neighbor, Finland, and subsequently forced the submission of Lithuania, Latvia, and Estonia. To many, the Soviet Union's aggression—and its alliance with Hitler—lent credence to the argument that Soviet communism was, after all, simply another face of fascism. With growing uneasiness Americans watched the events transpiring across the Atlantic. Many felt that the coun-

try should join the fight to protect democracy; others insisted that the United States should stay out of the battle.

Lillian Hellman eloquently expressed her opinion on this volatile issue in her new play, *Watch on the Rhine*. The drama opened at the Martin Beck Theater on April 1, 1941, just months before the United States entered World War II. About the play's timing, Hellman wrote, "There are plays that, whatever their worth, come along at the right time, and at the right time is the essence of the theatre and the cinema."

Set in an affluent Washington, D.C., suburb in the spring of 1940, *Watch on the Rhine* chronicles the political awakening of an American family. At the play's opening Sara Farrelly returns from Europe with her husband, Kurt Müller. Sara's family soon learns that

Londoners pass through a street devastated by German bombs in 1941. That same year Hellman's play Watch on the Rhine *exhorted Americans to go to war against the Nazis.*

Müller is a member of Germany's antifascist underground. As the plot unfolds, Müller is forced to kill an unscrupulous Nazi sympathizer in order to carry out his mission to free political prisoners held by the German government. Before Müller leaves Washington, he is able to convince his in-laws not to report the murder until he has had time to get out of the country. At the play's end the Farrellys realize that the war against fascism, which once seemed far away, has become their own. They have, as one family member describes it, been "shaken out of the magnolias."

Both the popular and critical response to *Watch on the Rhine* were highly enthusiastic, and the play ran for 378 performances on Broadway before going on tour. While later theater historians might consider it a heavy-handed melodrama, its immediate appeal lay in its powerful expression of the choices—both moral and political—that faced the United States on the eve of its entry into World War II.

Within a month of the play's opening Hellman was awarded her first New York Drama Critics Circle Award, the prize that had been created in response to the controversy over *The Children's Hour*. The following year *Watch on the Rhine* was selected for a command performance before President Franklin Delano Roosevelt. Soon afterward an illustrated limited edition of the play was printed and sold to benefit the Joint Anti-Fascist Refugee Committee, a charitable group in which Hellman was active. Finally, a film version of the play, adapted by Dashiell Hammett, was released and judged one of the best films of the 1943–44 season.

Hellman accepts a Drama Critics Circle Award for Watch on the Rhine. *The prize was created in response to the controversy over* The Children's Hour.

America entered World War II after Japan, a German ally, bombed the U.S. naval base at Pearl Harbor in December 1941. Although many might question their patriotism in the years ahead, both Hellman and Hammett were deeply committed to the war effort. The 48-year-old Hammett volunteered for army service in September 1942. And Hellman's passionate antifascism had not waned even when it conflicted with her loyalty to the Soviet Union: *Watch on the Rhine* exhorted Americans to rally against Hitler even though Germany was still a Soviet ally. In addition, Hellman volunteered for a number of projects to help the war effort. She wrote speeches for politicians and even delivered a few of her own.

Hellman feared that the repression, brutality, and anti-Semitism that characterized the Nazi regime might one day menace the United States. In a speech she gave in 1940, she proclaimed, "I . . . want to be able to go on saying that I am a Jew without being afraid of being called names or end in a prison camp or be forbidden to walk down the street at night. . . . Unless we are very careful and very smart and very protective of our liberties, a writer will be taking his chances if he tells the truth, for as the lights dim out over Europe, they seem to flicker a little here too."

In June 1941 Hitler made an abrupt about-face and, violating the nonaggression pact, invaded the Soviet Union. Betrayed by its former ally, the besieged USSR joined the fight against Germany. Because the Soviets now took the Allied side in the conflict, the Roosevelt administration wanted Hollywood to make a movie that would favorably influence U.S. public opinion on the Soviet Union. Hellman agreed to work on the project.

North Star was originally conceived as a documentary depicting the heroic struggle of ordinary Russian men and women against their Nazi invaders. It was to have been a collaborative effort between Hellman, director William Wyler, and producer Sam Goldwyn. However, Wyler left the project to enlist in the army and was replaced by director Lewis Milestone.

When the film was released in November 1943 Hellman's work had been radically altered, and the film had become a far less serious and realistic version of her screenplay. Although critics approved of its antifascist message, they complained that Milestone had glossed over the truth to create a romantic Hollywood epic. So strongly had Hellman objected to Milestone's changes that she bought out her contract with Sam Goldwyn and thus ended a working relationship that had lasted for eight profitable years.

In 1942 Hellman had started to write a second play about fascism but had put it aside to work on *North Star*. She finally completed her drama in 1943, and it opened on Broadway the following year. *The Searching Wind* expresses the playwright's conviction that cowardice and passivity fueled the spread of fascism across Europe and thereby led to World War II.

Montgomery Clift, Dennis King, and Cornelia Otis Skinner perform the final scene of The Searching Wind. *The provocative 1944 drama was Hellman's second play about World War II.*

The response to *The Searching Wind* was strongly divided. There was enough support for the play for it to lose the New York Drama Critics Circle Award by just one vote, and it ran for 318 performances. (Just 100 are needed for a play to be judged a commercial success.) Hellman's old friend, critic Louis Kronenberger, remarked that *The Searching Wind* "offers the kind of hard-hitting, genuinely adult writing that only Miss Hellman brings nowadays to the American theater." But other reviewers charged that Hellman had once again weighed down her drama with too much political content. At least two of the play's critics could not help dubbing it "more windy than searching."

With the blessing of the Roosevelt administration, Hellman traveled to the Soviet Union as a cultural ambassador in September 1944. She had been invited by Stalin's government, which was aware of her pro-Soviet sympathies. Her journey began with a train ride from Los Angeles to Seattle. She wrote Arthur Kober that the most eventful part of this trip was sharing a train compartment with "an interesting roach." Hellman might joke about the privations of this early leg of her travels, but less laughable discomforts were to follow.

From Seattle she went to Fairbanks, Alaska, where she was picked up by a Soviet flight crew. The trip to the USSR was made in a primitive two-engine plane whose heater broke soon after takeoff. Concerned about the safety of their illustrious passenger, the Soviet

Hellman boards a plane during a journey to the USSR. Acting as an informal ambassador, she toured war-torn Soviet cities and visited the World War II battlefront.

crew flew only in clear weather. When the weather was bad—as it often was—the crew stopped off at a series of shacks sprinkled across the frozen wastes of Siberia. By the time Hellman reached Moscow, 14 days after leaving Alaska, she had developed a case of pneumonia.

Because of her illness Hellman was invited to stay at the American ambassador's residence rather than at a hotel. After she recovered, she spent most of her time meeting with Russian and American officials, sightseeing, and working on the screenplay of *The Searching Wind*. As she reported in her memoir *An Unfinished Woman*, Hellman was moved by the courage of the Russian people, who had suffered greatly during the German invasion. She visited the city of Leningrad, which was recovering from a long siege. She also toured hospitals filled with wounded and dying soldiers. Perhaps her most emotional moment came during an inspection of the Maidanek concentration camp, which had been recently abandoned by the Germans. Hellman became physically sick after viewing the camp's death ovens and open graves.

During her months in the Soviet Union, Hellman became romantically linked with John Melby, a diplomat at the American embassy. The relationship lasted long after her return to the United States. Melby would suffer for his involvement with Hellman years later, during the anticommunist witch-hunts of the late 1940s and early 1950s. By that time her left-wing associations had made her so suspect that Melby's character was called into question simply because he had associated with her.

In January 1945, as the Soviet army pushed Nazi troops out of Poland and back into Germany, Hellman visited the front lines. Traveling with a Soviet batallion, she weathered German shelling and observed the questioning of captured Nazi soldiers. But two weeks on the front were enough for Hellman: She declined a Russian general's offer to accompany his army's triumphant march into Warsaw, Poland, and finally into the German capital of Berlin. Instead she returned to Moscow for a few weeks before flying to New York at the end of February. In March, she published an account of her experience in *Collier's* magazine. Her article praised the Soviets' "ability to speak about war, death, love and hate without self-consciousness and without fake toughness."

Within months of Hellman's return World War II ended in an Allied triumph. But the conflict's end did not, as many had hoped, usher in a period of international accord. In less than a year many nations were embroiled in a new and dangerous set of political tensions that came to be known as the cold war. The cold war's chief antagonists were the United States and the Soviet Union. Its contending ideologies were not democracy and fascism but capitalism and communism. Shortly, the conflict between the two superpowers would result in internal problems that would divide American society and lead to the persecution of communist sympathizers such as Hellman.

But these storm clouds had not yet appeared in the summer of 1945, as the war wound down and Hellman's life resumed its normal course. Hammett was discharged from the army that August and settled in at the Hardscrabble estate; Hellman embarked on a number of new projects. She completed the film adaptation of *The Searching Wind* and was disappointed when the movie opened to very poor reviews. She began work on a new play, *Another Part of the Forest*, the second of a proposed trilogy about the Hubbard clan portrayed in *The Little Foxes*. (Hellman never wrote the third play, saying that she had simply grown tired of the Hubbards.)

Another Part of the Forest (1946) was Hellman's second drama about her mother's family. After World War II, Hellman once again drew on more personal subjects for her plays.

The major conflict of *The Little Foxes* centers on the Hubbards' destructive obsessions with money and power; *Another Part of the Forest* takes the audience back a generation and attempts to explore the psychological origin of those obsessions. The first of 3 plays that Hellman would direct herself, *Another Part of the Forest* opened at the Fulton Theater on November 20, 1946, and ran for 191 performances. Compared to Hellman's other successful dramas, its run was among the briefest. Although some critics liked the play, others charged its author with relying on excessively melodramatic plot devices, including blackmail, theft, and bouts of insanity. Today's general assessment of *Another Part of the Forest* is that it is far inferior to its powerful predecessor, *The Little Foxes*.

For Hellman, the play's opening was marred by an event far more upsetting than mediocre reviews. Her father, Max Hellman, attended the premiere and spent the first act counting money and murmuring to himself. When intermission came, he announced to the other theatergoers, "My daughter wrote this play. It gets better." A few days later a concerned Hellman learned that her father was suffering from senile dementia. She was eventually forced to commit him to a mental hospital, where he died in 1948.

After *Another Part of the Forest* closed in April 1947 Hellman turned her attention away from the theater and toward her other ongoing interest, politics. The mounting antagonism be-

Actor and future president Ronald Reagan testifies before the House Un-American Activities Committee in 1947. Reagan supported HUAC's attempts to rid Hollywood of suspected communists.

tween the United States and the Soviet Union was beginning to have a domestic impact. FBI director J. Edgar Hoover had recently charged that communists were infiltrating every institution in American society, from the federal government to the movie industry. His accusations were heeded by the House Un-American Activities Committee (HUAC), which targeted the film industry for investigation. Committee members maintained that Hollywood needed a good "cleansing" and cited the pro-Soviet films made during World War II as proof of communist infiltration.

In September 1947 HUAC summoned scores of witnesses to answer questions about their political beliefs and the pervasiveness of communism in Hollywood. Some witnesses—stars such as Gary Cooper, Robert Taylor, and Ronald Reagan (then president of the Screen Actors Guild)—testified that communism was indeed widespread in the film industry. But other witnesses were less eager to cooperate with HUAC. Ten men simply defied the committee, refusing to answer questions and challenging HUAC's right to pry into individuals' political beliefs. Known as the Hollywood Ten, these defiant writers, directors, and producers were cited for contempt of Congress. They were subsequently indicted by a grand jury and sent to prison.

Reacting to the growing anticommunist fervor, Hollywood's studio heads issued a joint statement saying that they would fire any employees who refused to answer HUAC's questions or who were known communists. Thus began the policy of blacklisting—the denial of employment to anyone deemed politically unacceptable—that became an integral part of the political persecutions of the coming years. Equally important, the fate of the Hollywood Ten at the hands of HUAC, the

courts, and the studios paved the way for the period that came to be known as the McCarthy era.

Hellman's response to the HUAC hearings and to the studios' behavior was outrage. In December 1947 she penned an editorial entitled "The Judas Goats" for *Screen Writers Guild Magazine*. Her angry piece issued a call to arms as it voiced her opposition to the HUAC proceedings and those who cooperated with them: "They frighten mighty easy, and they talk mighty bad. For one week they made us, of course, the laughing stock of the educated and decent world. I suggest the rest of us don't frighten so easy. It's still not un-American to fight the enemies of one's country. Let's fight."

Hellman's exhortation seemed to fall on deaf ears, and she soon fell victim to the blacklist herself. The following year she was denied an opportunity to write the screen adaptation of Theodore Dreiser's novel *Sister Carrie* because the studio questioned her political loyalty. It would be nearly 20 years before she was again invited to write for Hollywood.

The threat of further personal harassment did not deter Hellman from participating in political activity. When former vice-president Henry Wallace ran for the presidency on the Progressive party ticket in 1948, she became one of his most active supporters. She headed a group called Women for Wallace and helped draft the Progressive party platform, which urged greater U.S.-Soviet cooperation, arms reduc-

Progressive party candidate Henry Wallace addresses supporters in 1948. Hellman backed Wallace's unsuccessful presidential bid and helped draft his party's liberal platform.

Hellman looks on as Soviet composer Dimitri Shostakovich speaks at the Waldorf Conference in 1949. The pro-Soviet meeting, held during the cold war, was quite controversial.

tion, and an end to the draft. Damaged by charges that the Progressive party was procommunist, Wallace received only 2.4 percent of the popular vote.

The autumn of Wallace's failed presidential bid found Hellman in Europe, where she interviewed Yugoslavian leader Marshal Tito. Tito had recently gained international attention by becoming the first communist leader to break publicly with the Soviet Union.

While abroad, she also met with playwright Emmanuel Roblés, whose play *Montserrat* would provide the basis for her next Broadway effort.

Back in the United States, in March 1949 Hellman became embroiled in yet another political controversy. She joined a number of other prominent artists and intellectuals—including Albert Einstein, Leonard Bernstein, and Frank Lloyd Wright—in hosting the

Cultural and Scientific Conference for World Peace. Held at New York City's Waldorf-Astoria Hotel, the gathering is often referred to as the Waldorf Conference. In sharp contrast to the prevailing anticommunism of the time, the conference promoted the idea of peaceful coexistence with the Soviet Union.

The gathering became the center of a heated controversy between pro- and anti-Soviet intellectuals. Many of its opponents charged that the Waldorf Conference was blatantly biased and simply another vehicle for spreading Soviet influence. Although he did not mention the Communist party by name, one of the few anti-Soviets invited to the meeting, magazine editor Norman Cousins, maintained that the gathering was serving "a small political group . . . which owes its allegiance not to America but to an outside govern-

A U.S. Air Force plane delivers food and supplies to Berlin. The airlift began in 1948, after Soviet troops blockaded the city in an unsuccessful attempt to gain control.

ment." His speech was greeted by a chorus of boos.

Hellman addressed the audience after Cousins left the podium. She admonished the angry crowd for its impoliteness. She could not, however, resist taking a jab at her anti-Soviet opponent: "I would recommend, Mr. Cousins, that when you are invited out to dinner, you wait until you get home before you talk about your hosts."

But Hellman's wit could not disguise the fact that Soviet expansionism was a reality: The USSR had recently backed a communist coup in Czechoslovakia and was attempting to take over Berlin by blockading the city. To the east, Mao Zedong, who had been supported by Stalin, was successfully completing a communist revolution in China.

The original cast plays a scene from Hellman's The Autumn Garden. *The 1950 drama—the playwright's personal favorite—received mixed reviews.*

While Hellman's politics may have been called into question, her talent as a playwright was not. The Moscow Drama Theater mounted a production of *Another Part of the Forest*; New York saw a presentation of composer Marc Blitzstein's opera *Regina*, based on *The Little Foxes*. Finally, on October 29, 1949, Hellman's latest work, her adaptation of Roblés's *Montserrat*, opened on Broadway. The play, set in 19th-century South America, explored whether or not individual lives could justly be sacrificed to further a revolution that might benefit millions. Although the play received mixed reviews, it exhibited Hellman's growing versatility as writer, director, and now, adapter.

This versatility was also demonstrated by her next original play, *The Autumn Garden*, which she began in the spring of 1950. In a marked departure from her recent works, Hellman turned away from political issues to focus on a group of individuals whose preoccupations and problems are purely personal. The play is set in a Gulf Coast summer resort. As the curtain rises, the audience is introduced to a group of characters, most of whom are middle-class and middle-aged. They are regular summer visitors at the resort, and most have grown up together. As the play's conflict emerges, the characters are forced to recognize that they had previously sidestepped some unpleasant truths about themselves. The irony of the belated self-discoveries is that they come at a time in the characters' lives when they no longer have the strength of will to change.

The critical response to *The Autumn Garden* was mixed. Some reviewers hailed the play, which opened at New York's Coronet Theater on March 7, 1951, as the playwright's most subtle and sensitive work. *Time* magazine praised the drama's "vividly drawn and brilliantly differentiated" characters. But the *New York Times* called it "boneless and torpid." *The Autumn Garden* closed after 101 performances— a respectable run, but a disappointing one for a play that Hellman considered her finest effort.

Hellman relaxes in her Manhattan town house. A few unsuccessful plays, coupled with political blacklisting in Hollywood, forced the writer to curtail her luxurious life-style in the 1950s.

SEVEN

Things Fall Apart

Lillian Hellman had turned away from politics to write *The Autumn Garden*, but political developments would soon have a profound effect on thousands of lives—Hellman's among them. In February 1950 a little-known Republican senator named Joseph McCarthy stood before an audience in Wheeling, West Virginia, and charged that the State Department had been infiltrated by communists. McCarthy told his startled listeners that he knew who these subversives were; in fact, he announced, he had a list of their names in his hand.

With this speech McCarthy launched himself onto the national stage by ushering in one of the most destructive episodes in American political history. During this period, often referred to as the McCarthy era, the U.S. Congress held scores of hearings at which indi-

viduals were asked to testify about their political activities and those of others. People who refused to answer these questions could be cited for contempt of Congress and sent to prison. Whether or not they were communists, those who chose to plead the Fifth Amendment—refusing to answer on the grounds that they might incriminate themselves—were branded as subversives and faced social ostracism and the loss of their jobs. Admitted communists could be prosecuted under the Smith Act, which declared it illegal to advocate the forceful overthrow of the government or to belong to an organization that advocated such an action. Blacklisting, which had been employed by the Hollywood studios since 1947, became a widespread practice. Some firms even hired alleged "specialists" to sniff out communists.

In July 1951 America's anticommunist hysteria invaded Hellman's personal life. Dashiell Hammett, a member of an organization that posted bail for individuals being prosecuted under the Smith Act, was sentenced to six months in prison for refusing to name the other contributors to the bail fund. According to Carl Rollyson, Hammett did not know the names of the other contributors. "But he refused to say even that much to a grand jury," Rollyson reported, "because he felt this would be cooperating with a system that used the Smith Act to persecute people not for their disloyalty, but for their unpopular opinions." During Hammett's imprisonment, the Internal Revenue Service (IRS) discovered that he owed over $100,000 in back taxes. From that point until his death in 1961, he was never again to be self-supporting, for all of his earnings went directly to the government to pay his tax debt.

Hellman, too, was having financial troubles. For the past two decades she had made a good deal of money as a playwright and screenwriter, but she spent her money as soon as she earned it. As Hellman herself noted, it is possible that she followed this pattern to compensate for the poverty of her

Joseph McCarthy (standing) testifies at a Washington hearing. The Republican senator's anticommunist witch-hunt touched hundreds of lives, including Hellman's.

Dashiell Hammett appears before the House Un-American Activities Committee. Because he refused to cooperate with HUAC, he was imprisoned for six months in 1951.

childhood, or to emulate the elegant way of life enjoyed by her mother's wealthy relatives. Whatever the reason, for most of her adult years Hellman had lived very comfortably, maintaining a farm in Westchester and a town house in Manhattan. She spent large sums traveling, entertaining, and indulging her taste for expensive clothes.

But by 1951 Hellman could no longer afford to live extravagantly. She had been blacklisted by Hollywood for the past three years and her most recent plays had not been commercial successes. Hammett's legal expenses had been staggering, and the IRS had recently found that Hellman, too, was in arrears on her taxes. For the first time since she became a self-supporting writer, Hellman was in financial trouble with no solution in sight. Seeing no alternative, she sold her beloved farm,

Hardscrabble, where she had lived for the past 12 years. Heartbroken by her loss, Hellman blamed the sale of the farm on persecution by the government.

Hammett was released from prison in January 1952; a month later Hellman herself was served with a subpoena to appear before the House Un-American Activities Committee. This summons could not have been unexpected. Spurred on by the mounting frenzy over communist subversion, HUAC had recently resumed its 1947 investigations into the movie industry. This time, however, the committee wanted the names of specific individuals who were or had been members of the Communist party. Even communist sympathizers, or "fellow travelers," were not spared public scrutiny. Scores of established and successful members of the Hollywood community were summoned before HUAC to repudiate their former activities and beliefs. They were also asked to name others who were, or may have been, members of the Communist party. In doing so, many of these witnesses betrayed past friendships and ideals to satisfy the committee in hopes of saving their reputations and careers.

One of the most cooperative witnesses to appear before HUAC in 1951 was screenwriter Martin Berkeley. Not only did Berkeley admit to his own past involvement in the Communist party, he also named 162 other members of the movie industry as communists or fellow travelers. One of those named was Lillian Hellman.

Hellman had long projected an image of herself—both in her work and in her political activities—as an outspoken fighter for justice and an unapologetic supporter of the Soviet Union. But when faced with the possibility of imprisonment for her beliefs, she became terrified. According to Joseph Rauh, the lawyer who represented her before HUAC, when Hellman visited his office for the first time, practical considerations merged with idealistic ones. "I will not go to jail," Hellman reportedly insisted. "I am not the kind of person who can go to jail. I do not want to plead the Fifth. It would make me look bad in the press. And I will not name names." With Rauh's guidance, Hellman devised a strategy that protected both her public image and her freedom. In a letter to HUAC dated two days before her scheduled appearance, she asserted her innocence of politically subversive activities and beliefs. She refused, however, to discuss the activities of others:

> I am not willing, now or in the future, to bring bad trouble to people who, in my past association with them, were completely innocent of any talk or any action that was disloyal. . . . To hurt innocent people whom I knew many years ago in order to save myself is, to me, inhuman and indecent and dishonorable. I cannot and will not cut my conscience to fit this year's fashions.

Hellman ended the letter by again expressing her desire to cooperate with HUAC—if she could confine her comments to her own beliefs and activities. She went on to say that if she was

HUAC questioned Hellman in May 1952. Two days before she testified, she wrote a letter to the committee stating: "I cannot and will not cut my conscience to fit this year's fashions."

Suspected communists known as the Hollywood Ten arrive at court in 1948. Hellman later regretted that she did not defy HUAC as these writers, producers, and directors had.

pressed to talk about the activities of others, she would be forced to claim the privilege of the Fifth Amendment.

As Hellman and Rauh expected, HUAC rejected her offer to testify only about herself, saying that it "cannot permit witnesses to set forth the terms under which they will testify." On the morning of May 21, 1952, Hellman appeared before a HUAC subcommittee. It was a brief encounter, lasting just over an hour. The committee's opening questions were routine: They asked her to state her name, place of birth, and occupation. Very quickly, however, the inquiry moved on to Berkeley's charge that Hellman was a Communist party member. In an early draft

84

of her letter to HUAC, Hellman had admitted to being a party member from 1938 to 1940. At her hearing, however, she refused to answer most questions about her involvement in the party, usually replying, "I must refuse to answer on the grounds that I might incriminate myself."

These replies would have probably marked Hellman as a "Fifth Amendment Communist" were it not for the letter she had submitted to HUAC. At one point in the hearing a committee member asked that Hellman's letter be entered into the record. With the letter now an official part of the hearings, Joe Rauh quickly rose and distributed copies to the press. The next morning, the *New York Times* carried the headline LILLIAN HELLMAN BALKS HOUSE UNIT. Because her letter implied that she was invoking the Fifth Amendment to protect others, not herself, many saw her as a woman motivated by loyalty, not self-preservation.

Unsure of how the public might react after her testimony, Hellman offered to bow out of her scheduled appearance as narrator at a performance of Marc Blitzstein's *Regina*. But Blitzstein insisted that her fears were unfounded and she must go through with the original plan. Resplendent in the same designer dress she had worn at the HUAC inquiry only a few weeks before, the nervous Hellman received a standing ovation from the crowd when she walked on stage for the performance. Blitzstein later reported that Hellman was so surprised that she looked behind

her to see if someone else was causing the uproar.

But Hellman's problems were not yet over. Many in the entertainment industry disliked her politics, Hammett's health was failing, and she still owed the IRS some $175,000 in back taxes. Additionally, diplomat John Melby, whom she had met in Moscow and continued to see after her return to the United States, was judged to be a security risk because of his relationship with her. As a result, he was fired and would never again work in the Foreign Service.

Desperately in need of money, Hellman chose a surefire hit for her next dramatic effort: She mounted a revival of her first play, *The Children's Hour*. Fortunately, unlike Hollywood, Broadway had never been seriously susceptible to blacklisting, and it remained a world in which Hellman had friends. The revival, which Hellman directed herself, opened at the Coronet Theater in December 1952, six months after her appearance before HUAC. The play could not have been more timely, for its dramatic depiction of the destruction wrought by innuendo and suspicion was a telling commentary on the American political climate of the time.

The Children's Hour revival was enthusiastically received and ran for 189 performances. Hellman's next money-making effort took her to Europe in 1953, where she wrote a screenplay for director Alexander Korda. Returning to the United States, she landed a job writing an introduction for and editing a collection of letters by the 19th-century Russian playwright Anton Chekhov.

Spring 1955 saw Hellman en route to Europe again, this time to London to see an English version of French playwright Jean Anouilh's drama about Joan of Arc, which Hellman was considering adapting for the American stage. Hellman saw possibilities in the play and flew back to the United States to find a translator and begin her adaptation. But work on the play was interrupted by yet another personal hardship: In August, Dashiell Hammett suffered a heart attack from which he never fully recovered. In the few years remaining to him, he was increasingly bedridden and dependent on Hellman.

Although much of her energy was devoted to caring for her longtime companion, in the fall of 1955 Hellman managed to complete her adaptation, entitled *The Lark*. With actress Julie Harris playing Joan of Arc, the play opened on Broadway on November 17, 1955. A *New York Times* headline summed up the critical reaction to the play: ALL CRITICS UNITE IN LAUDING "LARK." Hellman's latest effort was a solid hit. Its financial success enabled her to pay the IRS and buy a summer home on Martha's Vineyard, where she had vacationed the past two summers.

During the next three years only one Hellman work was produced on Broadway, a comic operetta based on *Candide*, the witty satire by 18th-century French writer Voltaire. The project was a collaborative effort between Hell-man, composer Leonard Bernstein, director Tyrone Guthrie, and poet Richard Wilbur. Despite the many talented people involved, the final product proved to be a fiasco, closing after 73 performances. Hellman later called her experience with *Candide* her most unpleasant experience in the theater. Perhaps this was because it was difficult for a person as strong-willed as Hellman to act as a team player.

After *Candide* closed in February 1957 Lillian Hellman began work on what would be her last original play, *Toys in the Attic*. With fitting symmetry, the idea for the play came from Dashiell Hammett, as had the concept for her first Broadway play, *The Children's Hour*. And just as she had drawn on the memories of her mother's family in creating the characterizations in *The Little Foxes*, Hellman reached back in time again for *Toys in the Attic*. But this time inspiration came from the early lives of her father and mother and from those of her aunts, Hannah and Jenny Hellman.

The setting for *Toys in the Attic* is the New Orleans boardinghouse of two middle-aged, unmarried sisters, Anna and Carrie Berniers, who have built their emotional lives around their younger brother, Julian. The two women believe that they want Julian to be rich and successful, but so far, he has failed at everything that he has tried. When Julian, with his neurotic young wife, Lily, arrives from Chicago with money and gifts, seeming finally to have "made good," the lives of all of the characters are turned upside down. As the play moves toward its climax, Lily ruins a pending business deal in the mistaken belief that Julian plans to leave her for another woman. Julian is once again rendered both penniless and helpless. Only then do the lives of the characters begin to resume their normal rhythms.

In its dramatic expression of the ways in which love can lead to dependency and destruction, *Toys in the Attic* is potent theater. Its opening at Broadway's Hudson Theater on February 25, 1960, was greeted with wide acclaim. The play ran for 556 performances, making it Hellman's most popular play after *The Children's Hour*. On May 19,

Hellman confers with composer Leonard Bernstein (center) and director Tyrone Guthrie, her collaborators on the 1956 comic operetta Candide.

Actors (left to right) Maureen Stapelton, Jason Robards, Irene Worth, and Anne Revere portray a scene from Hellman's 1960 hit, Toys in the Attic.

1960, *Toys in the Attic* earned Hellman her second Drama Critics Circle Award.

Not only was *Toys in the Attic* Hellman's last original play, it was also the last of her works to be seen by Dashiell Hammett. Hammett's health had deteriorated to the point where he was no longer able to live alone. By 1958 a concerned Hellman had convinced him to move into her Manhattan town house so that she could care for him.

On January 1, 1961, Hammett was hospitalized at Lenox Hill Hospital, where he died nine days later. In addition to inoperable lung cancer and emphysema, Hammett had suffered from a host of other painful complaints. At his funeral, Hellman spoke of Hammett as "a man of simple honor and great bravery." Her companion of 30 years was gone, and Hellman would miss him for the rest of her life.

Hellman's reputation soared in the early 1960s. She received scores of awards and honors and was asked to teach at two of America's top universities, Harvard and Yale.

EIGHT

Reinventing the Past

Lillian Hellman made a number of changes in her life after Dashiell Hammett's death. With the emotional and financial burden of Hammett's illness behind her, she started to freely indulge her taste for socializing with well-known actors, writers, and artists. As one longtime friend, set designer Howard Bay, explained it: "Hammett wouldn't let Lillian be a celebrity. When he died, she bought herself a new mink coat and really did it." She also began dating a number of men, most notably Arthur Cowan, a wealthy Philadelphia businessman.

Hammett's death also coincided with the beginning of Hellman's re-emergence as a nationally known literary figure. The success of *Toys in the Attic* was followed almost immediately by her election to the American Academy of Arts and Letters, a society

that distributes funds and grants to artists in all creative fields. In 1961 Hellman received achievement awards from three prestigious learning institutions: Wheaton College, Yeshiva University, and Brandeis University.

Her reputation as a writer also won her an invitation to serve as a visiting lecturer at Harvard University. Eager for a new challenge, she accepted the offer and taught creative writing in the spring of 1961. Although she questioned her credentials as an instructor—and was unsure if writing was a skill that could be taught—she proved to be an enthusiastic and inspiring lecturer.

While Hellman was at Harvard she read a novel by Burt Blechman that would become the basis of her last Broadway play. Entitled *How Much?*, Blechman's satire of Jewish family life reminded Hellman of her own childhood. For her adaptation the playwright added new characters and themes, creating an extensive indictment of middle-class America's obsession with money at the expense of moral values.

My Mother, My Father and Me opened on Broadway on March 21, 1963, and was a resounding failure, closing after only 17 performances. Almost all the reviews were extremely critical. Once again, the playwright was charged with attacking too many targets at the same time. Hellman believed that the play had merit but that flaws in writing and direction had damaged an otherwise good work. "I thought, and think now," she wrote in *Pentimento* years later, "that it is a funny play, but we did not produce it well and it was not well directed." After the failure of *My Mother, My Father and Me*, Hellman never again wrote for the stage. She would soon turn to another form, one in which she would reach her audience directly, without relying on directors and actors to convey her message.

Hellman's social activism had waned after her encounter with HUAC in the early 1950s, but she had not lost interest in political issues. In 1963 she went to Washington, D.C., to report for the *Ladies' Home Journal* on the historic civil rights march that drew a crowd of more than 200,000 supporters to the nation's capital. It was at this rally that Dr. Martin Luther King, Jr., delivered his best-known speech, in which he proclaimed, "I have a dream that this nation will rise up and live out the true meaning of its creed, 'We hold these truths to be self-evident; that all men are created equal.'"

Hellman was increasingly inspired by the American civil rights movement at a time when she was growing disillusioned with the Soviet Union. In 1965 she joined a number of other artists and intellectuals in writing a letter to Soviet premier Aleksey Kosygin protesting the arrest of Soviet writers who had published their works abroad. She also made two trips to the USSR, in 1966 and 1967, but her reactions to the country were more critical than they had been in the past. Hellman met with novelist Alexander Solzhenitsyn and other Soviet dissidents, praising their "fight for their own freedom to write as they wish to write." She later reported that her 1967 visit ended abruptly. Barred from addressing an official writers' congress because her speech was not approved by Soviet authorities, she angrily left the country.

Hellman's nearly 20-year absence from Hollywood ended when she returned to screenwriting in 1965 at the invitation of producer Sam Spiegel. She began work on a screen adaptation of Horton Foote's *The Chase*, a novel about violence in a small southern town. Hellman worked on the script for a number of months before submitting it to Spiegel. However, once it was out of her hands, her screenplay was turned into an awkward commentary on the 1963 assassination of President John F. Kennedy. Hellman complained to a *New York Times* reporter that

Hellman and director Gower Champion use models to plan the stage design of My Mother, My Father and Me. *The 1963 comedy, Hellman's last play, drew on her early life.*

Martin Luther King, Jr., delivers his stirring "I Have a Dream" speech at the August 1963 civil rights rally that drew 200,000 supporters— including Hellman—to Washington, D.C.

"what was intended as a modest picture about some aimless people on an aimless Saturday night got hot and large. . . . Well, it is far more painful to have your work mauled about and slicked up than to see it go in a wastebasket."

Hellman was involved in a variety of projects in 1966, the year *The Chase* premiered. She conducted a freshman seminar in literature and writing at Yale University in New Haven, Connecticut. As she had done at Harvard, she encouraged her students to strip their writing of flowery adjectives and to concentrate on strong, believable story lines. That same year she edited a collection of Hammett's writings entitled *The Big Knockover: Stories and Short Novels by Dashiell Hammett.*

The growing national recognition of Hellman's achievements as a playwright culminated on the night of October 26, 1967, with an all-star revival of her most celebrated play, *The Little Foxes.* The play was directed by Mike Nichols and featured Anne Bancroft, Margaret Leighton, and George C. Scott in key roles. The new production was hailed by critics from New York's most influential newspapers. Although it had been scheduled for a limited run of 100 performances, the audience response was so positive that the play moved from Lincoln Center to Broadway's Ethel Barrymore Theater for an additional 40 performances. After closing in New York, it began a successful national tour that solidified the play's reputation as an American classic.

A completely new career opened for Hellman with the 1969 publication of her first memoir, *An Unfinished Woman*. The book was a first-person narrative in which the author sketched selected aspects of her life. She wrote about her early years in New York and New Orleans, her experiences in Hollywood, and her visits to Spain and the Soviet Union. Hellman also rendered vivid portraits of several people who had been important to her: the writer Dorothy Parker; Hellman's housekeeper and friend, Helen Jackson; and Dashiell Hammett.

But the real hero of *An Unfinished Woman* is Lillian Hellman herself. Just as *Watch on the Rhine* had been perfectly suited to the World War II era, *An Unfinished Woman* captured the spirit of the feminist movement that emerged in the 1960s. The memoir painted a picture of an independent and courageous woman who was still struggling, at the age of 62, to define her own personality and place in the world. Not only did the book win praise for its literary quality, but the image of Hellman that emerged from its pages became a source of inspiration for millions of American women attempting to redefine their lives.

An Unfinished Woman became an immediate best-seller. Although some readers objected to Hellman's decision not to discuss her life in the theater—the arena in which her professional reputation had been made—the book was praised for its style and for its author's modesty and candor. On March 4, 1970, it received the National Book Award in the category of arts and letters.

Hellman stepped up her political activities in the late 1960s and early 1970s. In contrast to earlier days, her target was no longer fascism abroad but abuses at home. She was concerned by attempts then being made by the federal government, particularly the FBI, the CIA, and the Justice Department, to silence those who protested civil rights abuses and the country's involvement in the Vietnam War. As subsequent revelations demonstrated, burglaries, wiretapping, and outright blackmail were employed against many individuals, including Martin Luther King, Jr.

Hellman's response was to organize the Committee for Public Justice. The committee, which was made up of prominent individuals of all political persuasions, monitored government activities and warned citizens about possible threats to their freedom and privacy. According to cartoonist Jules Feiffer, one of those recruited, Hellman was the organization's prime mover: "She got on the phone and brought together a group of lawyers and professors and writers and statesmen and a millionaire or two and formed the Committee for Public Justice. She chaired the meetings, helped raise the funds, got others to raise more funds, thrashed out agendas."

The Committee for Public Justice was active from 1970 through 1982. During that time, Hellman held meetings throughout the country to win support for the organization and to publicize the government's infringements of civil liberties. In addition, the group's newsletter, *Justice Department Watch*, published reports of such abuses. The committee's activities, which were covered by both the national and international press, curtailed abuses of federal power, including wiretaps ordered by FBI Director J. Edgar Hoover.

With characteristic energy Hellman completed a second volume of memoirs while heading up the Committee for Public Justice. *Pentimento* was published in 1973 and was received even more enthusiastically than *An Unfinished Woman*. Not only did the volume remain on the best-seller list for more than four months, it was also chosen as a Book-of-the-Month Club selection.

Pentimento was divided into seven separate essays. "Bethe," "Willy," "Julia," and "Arthur W. A. Cowan" take as their subjects people who Hellman said were significant to her. The remaining three pieces focus on pivotal incidents and periods in the playwright's life. "Theater" describes her experiences as a dramatist. "Turtle" relates a humorous yet dramatic encounter between Hellman, Hammett, and a turtle that prompted a meditation on the meaning of life. The title essay, "Pentimento," is a recollection of the deaths of two people whom she loved, Dashiell Hammett and her housekeeper, Helen Jackson.

"Julia" is the most famous essay in the collection—and the one that would ultimately prove to be Hellman's undoing. The piece supposedly tells the story of her childhood friend and personal hero. "Julia" portrays a wealthy American heiress who, as a young woman, studied medicine in Vienna and joined the Austrian antifascist underground prior to World War II. According to Hellman's account, Julia was eventually captured, tortured, and killed by the Nazis, but not before she had inspired a modest act of heroism in Hellman. At Julia's request, the young playwright reportedly found the courage to smuggle $50,000 in cash from Paris to Berlin while en route to the Moscow Theater Festival in 1937. The money was to be used to help resistance fighters escape the Nazis.

In time "Julia" became Hellman's signature story, and the revelation of this previously unknown facet of her life added to Hellman's image as a courageous, complex, and modest woman. The account had so captured the public imagination that Hellman was offered $500,000 for the film rights to "Julia" and another *Pentimento* essay in 1976.

By the fall of 1976 a movie based on Hellman's memoirs was in the works. The film was produced by Richard Roth and directed by Fred Zinneman. But instead of a movie that combined two essays, the production focused solely on the "Julia" account. Vanessa Redgrave was hired to play the title role; Hellman's character was portrayed by Jane Fonda. The choice of the two actors was fitting, not simply be-

cause of their cinematic accomplishments but also because both were associated with controversial political issues: Redgrave was a supporter of the Palestinians in their struggle with Is-

Military police attack demonstrators protesting the Vietnam War. In 1970 Hellman formed the Committee for Public Justice to monitor such government abuses of civil rights.

rael; Fonda had been an outspoken critic of the United States's involvement in Vietnam.

As negotiations for the filming of Hellman's story were in progress, she published *Scoundrel Time*, the third installment in her trilogy of reminiscences. Many critics praised the book, which remained a best-seller for 23 weeks. *Scoundrel Time* is the only memoir in which Hellman addresses her political experiences at any length. Sidestepping the issue of her own pro-

Soviet activities and dismissing Stalin's political purges as mere "sins," *Scoundrel Time* focuses on her 1952 encounter with HUAC and presents Hellman as a lone fighter against political persecution. Hellman also attacks anticommunist liberals, who, she claimed, did not speak out against HUAC's persecutions or come to the defense of those like her who were under attack:

I had, up to the late 1940's, believed that the educated, the intellectual, lived by what they claimed to believe:

Jane Fonda (right) portrays Hellman in this scene from the 1977 film based on Hellman's memoir Pentimento. *Vanessa Redgrave (left) played* Julia's *title character.*

freedom of thought and speech, the right of each man to his own convictions. . . . But only a very few raised a finger when McCarthy and the boys appeared. Almost all, either by what they did or did not do, contributed to McCarthyism, running after a bandwagon which hadn't bothered to pick them up.

Hellman's charges would, in the months and years following the book's publication, provoke reassessments of the McCarthy era and inspire challenges to the accuracy of her version of events as well as to the image of herself conveyed in her memoir. Several critics angrily maintained that many anticommunist liberals did indeed oppose McCarthyism and that Hellman claimed otherwise largely to enhance her self-portrait as a woman alone fighting persecution. Critic Hilton Kramer also bristled at her glancing reference to Stalin's "sins," and pointed out that Hellman glossed over her naive loyalty to the Soviet leader who committed mass murder in order to carry out his goals. "Miss Hellman," he wrote, "was once one of the most vigorous public defenders of those 'sins' which even [Soviet premier] Khrushchev did not hesitate to call crimes."

While some critics were beginning to challenge Hellman's credibility, she still enjoyed a generally favorable reputation. In May 1976 Columbia University awarded her an honorary degree as an "illustrious woman of letters" who had not only made an invaluable contribution to the American theater of the 1930s and 1940s but who in recent years had continued to reflect the best values of civilization "through sensitive, candid, and finely written memoirs." Less than a year later, on the evening of March 30, 1977, the 71-year-old author, now quite frail and struggling against impending blindness, appeared as a presenter at the Academy Awards ceremony. She was introduced by Jane Fonda, who praised her for her literary achievement and for her "bravery in the face of political oppression."

Amid widespread publicity, *Julia* opened at movie theaters in October 1977. A beautifully made film, it received very positive early reviews and was praised for its affirmation of a long-lasting friendship between women. While later reviews were somewhat more critical, complaining of its "old-fashioned direction" and overglorification of the Hellman character, *Julia* was a box office success. By this time Hellman, in the words of writer Diana Trilling, had become "a heroine of culture."

But the next few years would bring new challenges to Hellman's heroic persona. The first salvo came in January 1980 on public television's "Dick Cavett Show." Cavett asked his guest, novelist and critic Mary McCarthy, about writers whom she considered overrated. McCarthy named, among others, Lillian Hellman, describing her as "a bad writer, overrated, a dishonest writer." She repeated a charge she had made against Hellman in a previous interview that "every word she writes is a lie, including 'and' and 'the.'" Hellman, who was watching Cavett's program that evening, responded with

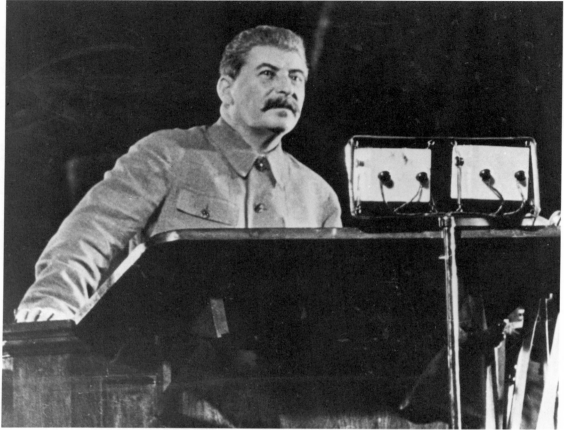

In her 1976 memoir Scoundrel Time, *Hellman discussed her politics for the first time. The book brought renewed criticism of her longtime support of the Soviet dictator Joseph Stalin (above).*

a $2.25 million lawsuit charging Mc-Carthy with defamation of character. The suit went on for years, ending only with Hellman's death.

Skepticism about Hellman's honesty was further fueled by the 1980 publication of her latest work, an autobiographical novella entitled *Maybe*. Ironically, the story's protagonist is a woman who lies. In *Maybe*, Hellman writes that a faulty memory—and personal feelings—can cause individuals to reshape their pasts. "But memory for all of us is so nuts," she wrote. "It's no news that each of us has our own reasons for pretending, denying, affirming what was there and never there." Some saw *Maybe* as a veiled confession that Hellman had made up or embroidered parts of her memoirs to make a political point or to suit her sense of dramatic style.

Because of the furor that arose from McCarthy's accusations and the publication of *Maybe*, writer Walter Clemons noted, "It is now open season on Hellman." Critic Vivian Gornick, for example, cast a suspicious eye on Hellman's earlier memoirs and asserted that "experience was being pushed around inside a stylishness of expression that should be taking orders, not giving them." The next major blow came in the spring of 1981, when the *Paris Review* published an article by journalist Martha Gelhorn. Ernest Hemingway's second wife, Gelhorn had been in Paris and Spain during the events described by Hellman in *An Unfinished Woman*. Gelhorn attacked the credibility of the memoir, particularly Hellman's account of the Spanish civil war. She cited her own recollections as well as public records to support her position. Again, Hellman was charged with both outright lies and distortions of fact.

Hellman's reputation suffered perhaps its greatest lashing when an autobiography entitled *Code Name: Mary* was published in 1983. The book was written by American psychiatrist Muriel Gardiner Buttinger, whose early life was nearly identical to Hellman's account of her friend Julia. The product of a wealthy family, Buttinger had been a student in Vienna, Austria, during the late 1920s. She had joined an anti-Nazi organization and carried out a number of dangerous assignments for the group. She eventually married Joe Buttinger, the leader of the Austrian resistance. In 1939 the two of them left Europe just as Hitler's armies invaded Poland. Later research documented both the truth of her account and the fact that she seemed to have been the only American woman in the Austrian underground.

In the introduction to *Code Name: Mary*, Buttinger said that many of her friends had insisted that she must have been the model for Hellman's Julia, but she rejected the idea because she and Hellman had never met. But as Hellman biographer William Wright points out, there was indeed a connection between the two women: Buttinger's lawyer and neighbor, Wolf Schwabacher, had ties to Lillian Hellman. He

Writer Mary McCarthy, above, accused Hellman of falsifying her memoirs. "Every word she writes," McCarthy asserted, "is a lie, including 'and' and 'the.'"

had tried to lift the Boston ban on *The Children's Hour* in the 1930s; he may also have been the vehicle through which Hellman learned of Buttinger's courageous life.

Buttinger's book created a furor, and increasing numbers of people became convinced that Julia and Buttinger were one and the same. It also seemed likely that she had been the model for other characters that had appeared in Hellman's writings, notably Sara Müller in *Watch on the Rhine*. However, when interviewed by a reporter for the *New York Times*, Hellman continued to deny that Buttinger had inspired her: "She may have been the model for somebody else's Julia," she snapped, "but she was certainly not the model for mine."

Hellman continued to deny the accusations against her as she herself grew increasingly preoccupied with more pressing matters. She had long been in deteriorating health and by 1982 she suffered from emphysema, severe arthritis, and nearly complete blindness. In addition, a recent heart attack had required Hellman to have a pacemaker installed. Nonetheless, she continued to work on several projects, including a book of recipes and recollections, *Eating Together*, which she wrote with her friend Peter Feibleman.

The ailing Hellman attempted to maintain some semblance of a social life, although her visits to restaurants and friends' homes were increasingly painful and awkward because of her infirmities. Her longtime friend, director William Wyler, recalled being amazed by her proud tenacity. "I made a note," he said, "to remember it. Because every day she did *something*. You would think that she would want to just relax, but no, every day she had them get her dressed, fix her hair, put a little makeup on her face, and she would go out." Flamboyant to the end, Hellman was not bothered by the spectacle she created as she was carried in and out of restaurants by attendants. As Wyler told biographer Carl Rollyson, "A slight hush would fall over the place and everybody would be whispering 'Who is that?' Of course she loved it."

On June 30, 1984, Lillian Hellman died of heart failure at the age of 79. The success of her plays and memoirs had left her a wealthy woman. Her will stipulated that much of her nearly $4 million estate be placed in 2 separate trust funds. The first was the Lillian Hellman Fund, which would award gifts and grants to selected applicants in the arts and sciences. The second was the Dashiell Hammett Fund, which would serve the same purpose—provided the qualified applicant's goals were in line with Hammett's Marxist views.

Of Hellman's own politics, which many found inexplicable in light of Soviet atrocities, perhaps fellow playwright Arthur Miller's assessment provides some insight:

What she feared more than untruth was fear itself; the main thing was always to defy. Her loyalty to the Soviet idea was on some level the same to her as loyalty to a friend. Integrity meant staying with the ship, even if it was veering in an unscheduled direction that would bring disaster to all the passengers.

Hellman's lifelong quest for moral absolutes may also have been behind the distortions that appear in her memoirs. Biographer Carl Rollyson calls Julia "a satisfying wish-fulfilling character" who embodies "everything Hellman was looking for: a person who would take personal responsibility for

Flanked by actors Maureen Stapelton and Elizabeth Taylor, Hellman receives an ovation on the opening night of a 1981 revival of The Little Foxes.

Although her reputation had been tarnished by attacks on her politics and character, when Lillian Hellman died on June 30, 1984, she was mourned as a fine writer and a courageous woman.

healing the world." Her sense of style may also have led her to embroider her memoirs. With her dramatist's flair, she seems to have reshaped her already extraordinary life to fit the standards of her art. As Richard Cohen remarked of Hellman in 1979, "She has truly become a legend in her own time and one reason is that she has lived long enough to help write it herself."

Whatever the outcome of the critical reassessment of her memoirs, Hellman's legend will live on long after her death. Her early work had a powerful impact on the American theater and paved the way for women dramatists in a male-dominated field. When Hellman launched her career, she expanded the traditional niche assigned to women dramatists, who were expected to write gentle, entertaining plays. Hellman's plays may have been entertaining, but her themes were socially and politically serious, her voice angry. Her dramas not only proved that women playwrights could address serious issues, they helped shape public opinion. The critiques of shallow values, cowardice, and duplicity she expressed in works such as *The Children's Hour* and *The Little Foxes* hit home with audiences—and continue to do so. Her plays, screenplays, and memoirs express the moral vision, intelligence, and combativeness that made Lillian Hellman one of the most influential and controversial women of the 20th century.

FURTHER READING

Estrin, Mark W. *Lillian Hellman: Plays, Films, Memoirs*. Boston: G. K. Hall, 1980.

Falk, Doris. *Lillian Hellman*. New York: Ungar, 1978.

Hellman, Lillian. *Eating Together: Recollections and Recipes*. With Peter Feibleman. Boston: Little, Brown, 1984.

———. *The Collected Plays*. Boston: Little, Brown, 1971.

———. *Maybe*. Boston: Little, Brown, 1980.

———. *Pentimento*. New York: Signet-NAL, 1973.

———. *Scoundrel Time*. Boston: Little, Brown, 1976.

———. *An Unfinished Woman*. New York: Bantam Books, 1970.

Lederer, Katherine. *Lillian Hellman*. Boston: Twayne, 1978.

Moody, Richard. *Lillian Hellman, Playwright*. New York: Bobbs-Merrill, 1972.

Riordan, Mary Marguerite. *Lillian Hellman: A Bibliography*. Metuchen, NJ: Scarecrow Press, 1980.

Rollyson, Carl. *Lillian Hellman: Her Legend and Her Legacy*. New York: St. Martin's Press, 1988.

Wright, William. *Lillian Hellman: The Image, The Woman*. New York: Simon & Schuster, 1986.

CHRONOLOGY

June 20, 1905	Lillian Hellman born in New Orleans, Louisiana
1911	Moves with parents to New York City
1922–24	Attends New York University and Columbia University
1924–25	Works as editorial assistant and manuscript reader for Boni and Liveright
1925	Marries Arthur Kober Dec. 31
1930	Moves to Hollywood; meets Dashiell Hammett
1932	Divorces Arthur Kober
1934	Hellman's first staged play, *The Children's Hour*, opens on Broadway
1936	*Days to Come* opens; *These Three* (film version of *The Children's Hour*) premieres
1937	Hellman writes screenplay for *Dead End*; travels to the Soviet Union and briefly visits Spain during the Spanish civil war
1939	*The Little Foxes* opens at New York's National Theatre
1941	*Watch on the Rhine* opens and wins the New York Drama Critics' Circle Award
1943	Hellman writes screenplay for *The North Star*
1944	*The Searching Wind* opens on Broadway
1945	Hellman travels to the Soviet Union as a cultural ambassador
1946	Film version of *The Searching Wind* premieres; *Another Part of the Forest* opens
1948	Hellman is blacklisted in Hollywood for her communist sympathies
1951	*The Autumn Garden* opens
1952	Hellman testifies before House Un-American Activities Committee
1960	*Toys in the Attic* opens and wins the New York Drama Critics' Circle Award
1967	*The Little Foxes* revived at Lincoln Center
1970	Hellman's first of three memoirs, *An Unfinished Woman*, wins National Book Award
1973	Hellman publishes *Pentimento*
1976	Publishes *Scoundrel Time*
1977	*Julia* (film adaptation of Hellman's memoir *Pentimento*) premieres in New York
1980	Hellman publishes *Maybe*, a novella
June 30, 1984	Lillian Hellman dies

INDEX

AP/Wide World, pp. 46, 73, 75, 101;   The Bettmann Archive, pp. 21, 23, 30, 35, 38, 41, 87;   Culver Pictures, pp. 2, 14, 16, 31, 34, 39, 40, 42, 44 (left), 49, 54, 58, 67, 83;   The Museum of the City of New York, Theatre Collection, pp. 62, 78, 88;   The National Archives, p. 64; The Historic New Orleans Collection, Museum/Research Center, Acc.# 1975.325.5221, p. 20;   New York Public Library at Lincoln Center, Astor, Lenox and Tilden Foundations, Performing Arts Research Center, pp. 12, 58, 70, 76, 90;   New York Public Library, Local History and Geneology Collection, pages 24, 27;   State Historic Society of Wisconsin, p. 18;   University of Southern California, Special Collections, p. 44 (right);   UPI/Bettman Newsphotos, pp. 15, 26, 28, 32, 50, 51, 52, 55, 57, 65, 68, 71, 74, 80, 81, 84, 93, 94, 97, 98, 100, 103, 104;   Wisconsin Center for Film and Theater Research, pp. 33, 36

Saundra Towns is a writer, critic, and lecturer in English at Baruch College, City University of New York. She is currently working on her doctoral degree in English at the City University Graduate Center.

❖   ❖   ❖

Matina S. Horner is president of Radcliffe College and associate professor of psychology and social relations at Harvard University. She is best known for her studies of women's motivation, achievement, and personality development. Dr. Horner serves on several national boards and advisory councils, including those of the National Science Foundation, Time Inc., and the Women's Research and Education Institute. She earned her B.A. from Bryn Mawr College and Ph.D. from the University of Michigan, and holds honorary degrees from many colleges and universities, including Mount Holyoke, Smith, Tufts, and the University of Pennsylvania.